24 TANDEM BIBLE STORYSCRIPTS

for CHILDREN'S MINISTRY

Steven James

Standard
PUBLISHING

CINCINNATI, OHIO

Dedication

To Mike, who found a Rock in the middle of the storm.

Thanks & Acknowledgments

This book is the result of ideas that grew and developed over many years. It would be impossible to individually thank all the preachers who have inspired and challenged me, all the storytellers who have taught and coached me, all the listeners who have laughed and encouraged me, and all the editors who have kindly and thoughtfully redirected me. So if you fall into any of those categories, thanks! This book is for you.

A few people come to mind whom I'd like to thank for special help on this series. Thanks to Ruth Frederick and Paul Learned for their friendship and their encouragement to think outside the box; to Bruce Stoker for his insightful suggestions on what stories to include in each volume; to Pamela Harty, for believing in me; to Terry Maughon and the staff at Doe River Gorge Ministries for giving me a place to think, write, tell stories, and talk to my wolf; to Dana Standridge for her tireless typing, attentive research, and insightful editing; and to my wife and daughters, for their extraordinary patience and delightful ideas.

Standard Publishing, Cincinnati, Ohio 45231
A division of Standex International Corporation

09 08 07 06 05 04 03   7 6 5 4 3 2 1
ISBN: 0-7847-1320-0

Edited by Bruce E. Stoker and Lindsay Black
Cover design by Joel Armstrong
Cover and interior illustrations by Paula Becker
Interior design by Dale Meyers

Table of Contents

Part 1—Tips, Tricks, and Techniques for Telling Tandem Tales

How to Use This Book 4

Keys to Effective Tandem Storytelling 5

How to Develop Your Own Tandem Stories 7

Part 2—Old Testament Stories

1. The World's First Artist 8

2. The Day Sin Came In 13

3. Cain Wasn't Abel 17

4. The Flood 20

5. The Dreamer *(the story of Joseph, act 1)* 25

6. The Rise of Zappo *(the story of Joseph, act 2)* 28

7. The Family Reunion *(the story of Joseph, act 3)* 33

8. The Kayak Kid 37

9. The Master of Disasters 41

10. The Giant Match-up 45

Part 3—New Testament Stories

11. Unidentified Flying Angels 48

12. The Missing Mini-Messiah 51

13. The Baptism of Jesus 55

14. No Dessert in the Desert 58

15. A Graveyard Story 60

16. www.greatbigfishcatch.net 62

17. Rappelling Through the Roof 65

18. The Last Supper 68

19. At the Scene of the Grave 70

20. Tongues of Fire 73

21. When Tabitha Got Sew Sick . . . She Dyed 76

22. Dinner Reservations 79

23. Who Can That Be Knocking at My Door? 81

24. The Breaking Jail Jailbreak 85

Scripture Verse Index 89

Story Type Index 91

Topical Index 92

How to Use This Book

Kids love stories. And they especially love it when stories are told in a humorous, lively, and engaging manner. The selections in this book will help you tell God's story to your students with creativity, humor, and fun audience participation.

These stories are written for live presentation. They could be performed using two onstage storytellers, a live person onstage talking to a puppet, or two puppeteers. Here are a few suggestions for making the most of this book.

Do we have to memorize these stories?

While the stories are written to be told, they will also work well read aloud. The style of presentation in which you dramatically read your parts is known as "reader's theater." It can be a very effective storytelling technique, as long as you look up at the audience when you're not reading, and make frequent eye contact with your students while you perform your part.

If you choose to read a story rather than tell it, photocopy the pages and place the sheets in a black folder so you're not reading from a book when you present the story to your students (permission to photocopy is granted for this purpose only).

How much can I change the wording of these stories?

Because of the interpersonal aspect of storytelling, storytellers need to be able to use language that's comfortable and natural for them. Even though great care has been taken in crafting the language of the stories in this collection, you may find that sometimes a slightly different wording sounds more natural to you.

Feel free to make minor editorial changes to the scripts in this book. You may wish to leave out a joke that wouldn't make sense to your listeners, or delete a phrase that might be misunderstood. (However, permission is not granted to alter the stories in such a way that you change the theological meaning or intent of the story.)

Do we need special costumes or props?

Unless otherwise noted, no special costumes are needed for the stories. However, you may wish to use some silly costumes for various characters or stories.

Use general stage lighting and two lapel microphones.

In most of these stories, one of the storytellers is more serious, while the other storyteller acts somewhat goofy. If you meet regularly with the same group of students, you may wish to have the same people (dressed in memorable or distinctive costumes) tell stories as these characters. The students will look forward to seeing the funny characters again and again! (If you use a puppet for only one of the characters, let the puppet play the role of the goofier storyteller.)

What kinds of stories are in this book?

Here are the six different presentation methods you'll find in this collection:

#1—Tandem Storytelling *(two storytellers alternate telling a story)*

When two storytellers take turns telling the same story, we say that the story is told in "tandem." Most of the stories in this book are tandem stories.

First and most common are stories in which one of the storytellers gets mixed up while the other storyteller tries to get everything right. In these stories you'll find lots of banter and verbal exchanges between the storytellers. The results can be hilarious!

A second style of tandem telling is more directed at the audience and has the storytellers alternating lines as the tale is delivered. Sometimes, the tellers even say their lines together. As you prepare these stories, read through the scripts carefully and work on your timing so that those sections don't sound mumbled.

#2—Tandem Monologues *(both storytellers deliver a monologue)*

When a storyteller tells the entire story from the point of view of one of the characters in the story, she is telling a "monologue." When performing tandem monologues, two storytellers take turns delivering their monologues.

Sometimes, both storytellers may be portraying the same person at different points in her life. For example, one storyteller may be telling Ruth's story from her perspective when she is a grandmother, while the other storyteller may be portraying Ruth as a young woman.

Tandem monologues can also be told from different peoples' perspectives. For example, one storyteller may tell the story of Jesus' death from the perspective of one of the shocked disciples, while the other storyteller tells the story from the perspective of one of the Roman soldiers.[1]

Typically, when delivering tandem monologues, the storytellers look only at the audience rather than at each other while telling the story.

#3—Narralogue (one person narrates, the other delivers a monologue)

Typically when a person tells a story, she includes both narration and dialogue. In other words, she might say, "Once upon a time there was a man named Elijah." That's *narration*. Then, she might say, "Elijah said to the widow of Zarephath, 'Please get me some food and water. I'm very hungry.' But she said, 'I have nothing to give you!'" The places where she portrays the voice, posture, and mannerisms of the characters while delivering her lines are sections of *dialogue*.

Some of the stories in this collection are arranged so that one of the storytellers does all (or nearly all) of the narration, while the other storyteller delivers the dialogue of the characters. I've called these stories "narralogues."

#4—Storymime (one person tells the story, the other acts it out)

With this type of tandem tale, one person serves as the primary storyteller, while the other storyteller does the actions (or shows the emotions) of the characters or events in the story. The speaking storyteller pauses after every action verb to allow time for her partner to act out what's happening in the story. (Suggested actions are included in the storymime scripts included in this book.)

If you desire, you can invite the children to imitate, or "mime," the actions after the silent storyteller has performed them. In that case, the storyteller who is relating the story must wait long enough for all the children to do their parts before continuing. (Be sure to explain what you'd like the students to do before beginning your story.)

In some stories, the silent storyteller may just put on an imaginary mask that portrays the emotions being felt in the story. Examples and suggestions are provided for the stories which incorporate this technique.

#5—Interview (one person interviews an eyewitness to the story)

A few of the scripts in this book portray interviews in which a detective or reporter arrives on the scene of an important biblical event and then interviews one of the characters from the story. For this type of story, it's fun to dress the part and wear crazy costumes!

#6—Sports Announcer (both storytellers report as if watching the story live)

Finally, both storytellers can pretend they are sports announcers and are reporting live from the scene of a famous Bible event. Once again, it can be fun to dress the part and act as if you really are announcing a game on TV.

---

1. For more detailed information on using and developing monologues, see pages 77-78 in my book *The Creative Storytelling Guide for Children's Ministry* (Standard Publishing, 2002).

Keys to Effective Tandem Storytelling

Tandem storytelling is a fun and effective teaching tool, but it can seem difficult to master at first. Here are five keys to effective tandem storytelling to help you get started.

Key #1—Strive for Believable Characterization

As you begin to prepare your story for telling, read through the script and become familiar with the personality of each storyteller. Then, consider who best fits the role for that character—you or your storytelling partner. One of the storytellers often ends up getting things mixed up. If you tend to be a natural class clown or if you like to ham it up, that's probably the part for you!

The closer your personality is to the personality of the storyteller in the script, the more natural the story will sound. On the other hand, it can be fun to take on an unexpected role. If your students expect you to be serious, you could be the goofier storyteller, but if they're used to seeing you act silly all the time, you might take on the more serious role.

Whichever part you choose, try to step into the persona of the character you're portraying so that you act *as if you were* that person, rather than just *like* that person. For example, if you're portraying Goliath in a story, you don't want to act "like a giant," but rather *as if you truly were Goliath and you're just being yourself.* It's a subtle difference, but it will help you create more believable, natural-sounding, and genuine characters.[2]

Key #2—Respond Naturally to Your Partner

Remember that old Abbot and Costello radio sketch called "Who's On First?" Remember how hilarious it was when Lou Costello kept getting mixed up, exasperated, and more and more confused? Those two comedians were a true team, playing off each other and responding perfectly to what the other person said.

When you tell a story with a partner, you want the delivery to be so seamless that it feels like a unified whole rather than an awkward combination of two people's parts. To achieve this unity, respond naturally and genuinely to your partner's words and actions. In other words, rather than sounding "rehearsed" or "canned," the story should sound like it's being told for the first time—every time you tell it!

Key #3—Listen to Your Partner

Listen to three things when you tell your story: (1) the flow of the story, (2) your storytelling partner, and (3) yourself. Really *listen* rather than just plowing forward with "your lines."

Work together as you learn the story rather than taking the scripts home and "memorizing" them separately. There may be times when your partner forgets a line or accidentally skips to the wrong place in the story. The more you practice together, the more naturally you'll be able to cover for that person and get the story back on track.

Also, the more you work with a specific partner, the more you'll be able to anticipate what that person will say, how she will say it, and how best to respond. All of this requires careful listening and attention.

Key #4—Keep the Story Moving Forward

As you work on your story you'll notice that sometimes the exchange between the two storytellers is quick—each line may be only one or two words. During these rapid-fire exchanges, be quick responding to each other, almost cutting each other off.

Listen to the story as you work on it to make sure that the story flows and the timing of the piece works to your advantage. It's no help to anyone if your students get bored. Instead, make sure that the pace, pauses, and timing of the story serve to enhance rather than distract from the presentation.

Key #5—Avoid Distractions

A storyteller typically looks at whomever he or she is addressing. If you're saying lines that are directed at your partner, look at her. But if you're narrating a section of the story to the audience, focus your attention on your students instead.

When your partner is saying her lines, don't draw attention away from the story by pacing, swaying, fiddling with your hair, or doing other annoying mannerisms.

If you're delivering tandem monologues, freeze and stare into the distance or at the audience (rather than looking at your partner) while your partner says her part. If you're performing a tandem story, look naturally at your partner whenever she is speaking, in order to focus the attention of the audience on her.

Summary

Good storytellers take the time to prepare their stories, but are also willing to be spontaneous and responsive to their listeners. As you tell your stories, remember to face the audience and use plenty of facial expressions, sound effects, and natural gestures. Make sure the students can hear you and won't be distracted by other things going on in the room. Have fun and let the story flow out of who you are rather than trying to imitate someone else. For more extensive tips on storytelling, see my book, *The Creative Storytelling Guide for Children's Ministry* (Standard Publishing, 2002).

---

2. Thanks to Dick Major and Tony Montanaro for their insights into acting and storytelling. I'm indebted to them for their explanations on the keys to effective acting.

How to Develop Your Own Tandem Stories

Begin with prayer. Pray that God will guide and direct your efforts to present his word in a unique, creative, and memorable way. Pray also that the students will be drawn closer to him as a result of your work. And remember, God always hears and answers prayers that promote his kingdom.

Then, become familiar with the story. Strive to understand the framework and the structure of the story. Ask yourself: *Who are the main characters? What is the struggle or problem presented in the story? What do the characters learn as a result of facing that struggle? How are their lives different at the end of the story from the way they were at the beginning?*

Remember that every story needs tension. If nothing goes wrong, you don't have a story, only a list of events. Sometimes tension is created because one of the storytellers keeps getting things mixed up. Sometimes humorous tension results from a misunderstanding of the significance of the story or of its application today. In stories told from the point of view of one of the characters, the tension comes from either an internal struggle (an unanswered question) or an external struggle (an unfinished task).

Look for shifts in time and place as you study the story. Look for sections of repetition or for things that just don't seem to fit. Consider how you'll approach story sections that may not be age-appropriate for your students. Are those sections integral to the story? Can you still be faithful to the text (and tell the story as God wants it told) by leaving out those sections? Extremely violent sections can be left out completely, or can be dealt with by exaggeration or humor.

Once you're familiar with the story you wish to retell, decide on a presentation style. Choose from the six options listed in the introduction: tandem storytelling, tandem monologues, narralogue, storymime, interview, and sports announcer.

Then, begin working on a first draft of your story. Jot down ideas as you say the story aloud rather than trying to listen to it all in your head or furiously write it all out on paper right away. Focus on speaking the story into existence.

Then begin a rough draft of the story. But once again, don't get too attached to the first draft. Avoid the temptation to "polish" your story too early in the process of developing it. Since the story is being written to be *told* rather than *read* silently, it's important to say the words so that you can understand how they flow together, when pauses and interruptions naturally occur, and whether or not the pace of the story is effective. Finally, as you write your story, remember to:

1. Only include dialogue that moves the story forward. Remove all unnecessary words.

2. Make each person's part brief. Eliminate long sections of one person talking. That can get boring fast.

3. Make the language informal and casual rather than stiff and "proper-sounding."

4. Be sure that each character's personality is revealed through her choice of words. Then, verify that her character remains consistent throughout the story. Include memorable phrases, clichés, or mannerisms for each character.

5. Use humor, but don't overdo it. Move the story along; don't stall out "trying to be funny." Be serious when making an important point or drawing to the close of the lesson.

6. While you practice your story, explore your blocking (i.e. where you stand and move during the story) and your gestures. Let the story grow as you discover new gestures or movements that add to your presentation. Let the story develop as you practice it rather than trying to rehearse it one specific way.

7. Let your storytellers do or say unexpected things in order to snag and keep the attention of listeners. If things become too predictable, your listeners will lose interest.

The World's First Artist

Based On:	Genesis 1-2
Big Idea:	God created the universe and made human beings in His own image.
Background:	Even though Christians don't all agree on the specific time frame of the earth's creation, they do agree that God is the creator of the universe. This story will help your students understand the love and creativity of God, the world's first Artist.
Type:	Tandem storytelling (with optional audience participation)
Tellers:	Bonnie—A serious storyteller trying to tell the story correctly (female or male); George—Her friend, who keeps getting everything mixed up (male or female).
Tools:	A flashlight, a loaded squirt gun (if desired), stuffed animals (such as fish, birds, werewolf), a surfboard (if desired)
Topics:	Creation, God's existence, God's power, rest
Tips:	If desired, teach the students the refrain and invite them to join along whenever George repeats it throughout the story. Both storytellers start onstage, or enter together. Bring up the stage lights, and then begin when the students are quiet.

Script

(Day 1)

Bonnie: Long ago—

George: Before there was anything else,

Bonnie: There was God.

George: And he decided to create a world!

Bonnie: Now, before he made the world, the earth was formless—

George: Like a great big glob of goo!

Bonnie: Right.

George: All gross and disgusting and slimy—

Bonnie: Well, something like that. And God said,

George: "Hmm.... Looks like play dough. I think I'll make a world."

Bonnie: Nope, before he made the world, he said…

George: *(Pulling out a flashlight)* Let there be light! *(Shine in Bonnie's eyes)*

Bonnie: Um. God didn't use a flashlight.

George: Why not?

Bonnie: He didn't have to. He could just use his mouth!

George: He used his mouth as a flashlight?

Bonnie: No, he used his mouth to say, "Let there be light!" That's all it took! And as he said it, light appeared. And after he'd made light, God said—

George: "Let there be light bulbs!" *(Hold up the flashlight again)* And flashlights!

Bonnie: No, God said, "Good! Good! My light is good! It's just the way I like it, my light is good!" Try it.

George:	"Good! Good! My light is good! It's just the way I like it, my light is good!"
Bonnie:	Okay.
George:	"Good! Good! My light is good! It's just the way I like it, my light is good!"
Bonnie:	That's enough.
George:	"Good! Good! My light is good! It's just the way I like it, my light is good!"
Bonnie:	Alright!
George:	That's kinda catchy.
Bonnie:	Thank you.
George:	You're welcome.
Bonnie:	Then, God called the light—
George:	"Duracell."
Bonnie:	No.
George:	"Eveready?"
Bonnie:	He called the light "day" and the darkness he called "night."
George:	Oh.
Bonnie:	And together, light and night made up one day . . . .
George:	"Good! Good! My day is good! It's just the way I like it, my day is good! Good! Good! My flashlight is good! It's just the way I like it, my flashlight is good!"

(Day 2)

Bonnie:	On the second day, God pushed some water up and some water down. And he called the space between them—
George:	Did you say water?
Bonnie:	Yes…
George:	Oh.
Bonnie:	And he called the place where the waters were—
George:	*(Pull out a squirt gun and spray Bonnie and the audience)* The squirt gun!
Bonnie:	Ah! Stop that! No, he called the space between them "sky." And then God said—
George:	"Good! Good! My sky is good! It's just the way I like it, my sky is good. Good! Good! My squirt gun is good! It's just the way I like it, my squirt gun is good!"

(Day 3)

Bonnie:	Right. And on the third day, God said, "Let's see some oceans!" and he gathered all the waters together in different places to make seas and rivers and oceans.
George:	*(Pull out squirt gun)*
Bonnie:	But not squirt guns.
George:	Too bad. . . . Did he make lakes and puddles and streams?
Bonnie:	Yes.
George:	Brooks and ponds and icebergs?
Bonnie:	Uh-huh.
George:	Estuaries, viaducts and marshland?
Bonnie:	Huh?
George:	Did God make waves?
Bonnie:	Well, yeah. I guess so.
George:	Did he make a splash!?

Bonnie:	Yeah.
George:	*(Optional—pull out a surfboard)* And surfboards!
Bonnie:	He did not make surfboards.
George:	Oh. Too bad.
Bonnie:	But he did make land and he also made all kinds of plants and trees and flowers.
George:	"Good! Good! My plants are good! They're just the way I like 'em, my plants are good!" *(Jump on surfboard)* "Good! Good! The surfing is good! It's just the way I like it. The surfing is good!"

(Day 4)

Bonnie:	Then on the fourth day, God made the sun and the moon and the stars and the planets in the sky. And God made the moon to shine at night and the sun to shine during the day—
George:	*(Interrupting)* Wait a minute, if he didn't make the sun 'til day four, how could there be day and night on day one?
Bonnie:	Well, remember, he already had light and darkness. He knew what a day was, he just hadn't put the light in a sun or a star yet.
George:	But how could that be? How could he do that?
Bonnie:	He is God.
George:	Oh, yeah. Right. "Good! Good! My stars are good! They're just they way I like 'em, my stars are good!" *(Optional—hand out star stickers)*

(Day 5)

Bonnie:	On the fifth day, God made fish and eels and dolphins and sharks—
George:	And sea monsters! Ah!
Bonnie:	Not sea monsters, but sea turtles and then God made the birds.
George:	Cawk! Cawk!
Bonnie:	Right!
George:	And God said, "Good! Good! My fish are good! They're just the way I like 'em! My fish are good!"
Bonnie:	Right!
George:	"Good! Good! My birds are good! They're just the way I like 'em! My birds are good!"
Bonnie:	You got it!
George:	"Good! Good! My sea monsters are good! They're just the way I like 'em! My sea monsters are good!"
Bonnie:	Oh, brother.
George:	Hee. Hee. Hee.

(Day 6)

Bonnie:	On the sixth day, God made cows and horses and pigs and—
George:	Werewolves.
Bonnie:	There were no werewolves!
George:	Vampires! *(Talking like a vampire)* I vant to suck your blood!
Bonnie:	Would you stop already!
George:	Okay.
Bonnie:	No, all the land animals and people, too.
George:	And the bogeyman.
Bonnie:	God didn't create the bogeyman!

George:	Then who did?
Bonnie:	Nobody!
George:	Oh. "Good! Good! My animals are good! They're just the way I like 'em! My animals are good! . . . Good! Good! My werewolves are good. They're just the way I like 'em! My werewolves are good!"
Bonnie:	No, people.
George:	Oh. Good! Good! My bogeymen are good—
Bonnie:	No. "Good! Good! My people are good! They're just the way I like 'em! My people are good!"
George:	Right. And so are my bogeymen.

(Day 7)

Bonnie:	Finally, on the seventh day—
George:	God slept in.
Bonnie:	Well, kind of.
George:	He did?
Bonnie:	Well, he rested on that day.
George:	He took a nap.
Bonnie:	Well, sort of.
George:	Was he tired?
Bonnie:	God doesn't get tired!
George:	Then why'd he sleep?
Bonnie:	He didn't sleep. He rested on that day to enjoy all that he had made. And he called it the most special day of all because—
George:	There was no school!
Bonnie:	Um, not exactly. It was a day set apart for renewal and enjoyment and rest from our work.
George:	And from school.
Bonnie:	Well, yeah.
George:	Cool. . . "Good! Good! My rest is good! It's the way I like it! My rest is good!" *(Pretend to fall asleep)* Zzzzz. . .
Bonnie:	*(To the audience, as George sleeps)* So, just like a painter, God first made sure he had enough light. Then, he got the canvas ready.
George:	*(Waking up)* By separating the waters from the sky?
Bonnie:	That's right.
George:	And making the dry land and the oceans?
Bonnie:	Uh-huh. And then, he started adding color.
George:	By making the trees and plants and flowers!
Bonnie:	Right! And then he filled the sky with lights! Stars and the moon and the sun so the background for his masterpiece would look just right.
George:	And then came the details!
Bonnie:	Yes! He filled his canvas with the best products of his imagination.
George:	Sea monsters and werewolves!
Bonnie:	Um, No.
George:	Fish and birds?
Bonnie:	Yeah, and then the land animals.
George:	Wow!
Bonnie:	And finally, he put the finishing touches on his masterpiece and stepped back to admire it.

George:	I never thought of all that before.
Bonnie:	Lots of times in the Bible God describes himself as "the Creator." And we're made in his image.
George:	We're artists, too?
Bonnie:	Some of us. And some of us are writers. Others are quarterbacks or violin players or comedians or dancers. . . . But all of us have this incredible thing called imagination.
George:	It's a gift of God!
Bonnie:	Yup. It helps us see what doesn't exist yet, and make it into a reality.
George:	Cool!
Bonnie:	And God looked at all he'd made and he said—
George:	*(Dramatically)* "Yeah, baby. That's good! . . . Good! Good! My world is good! It's just the way I like it! My world is good!"
Bonnie:	Close enough.
Together:	The end.

(Bow. Fade out the stage lights. As the storytellers exit, George sings, "Good! Good! My sea monsters are good! They're just the way I like 'em. My sea monsters are good!")

The Day Sin Came In

2

Based On: Genesis 3

Big Idea: Adam and Eve chose to disobey God and, because of their choice, sin entered the world. Yet through it all, God still showed them compassion and grace.

Background: Sometimes when people read the story of Adam and Eve, they think God wasn't fair in how he treated his newly created people. Why would he create a tree that could cause them death? Why didn't he just overlook their one "little mistake"? And why did he call out for them; couldn't he tell where they were? This script addresses some of these questions and demonstrates that God continued to treat his children with justice, mercy, love, and compassion.

Type: Tandem storytelling

Tellers: Bonnie—A serious storyteller trying to tell the story correctly (female or male); George—Her friend, who keeps getting everything mixed up (male or female).

Tools: None

Topics: Choices, consequences, death, demons, excuses, faith, forgiveness, God's love, grace, hiding, obedience, second chances, sin, temptation

Tips: Both storytellers start onstage, or enter together. Bring up the stage lights, and then begin when the students are quiet.

Script:

Bonnie: *(To the audience)* Today, I have a really exciting story to tell you.

George: It's a story about Adam.

Bonnie: And Eve.

George: And the choice that they made one day long ago,

Bonnie: In the Garden of Eden. Now, the snake—

George: *(Emphasizing the "s" sounds)* SSSSSSSSSSSSSSSSSS—was the s-s-s-sneakiest, s-s-s-slitheries-s-s-st, shrewdes-s-s-st, s-s-s-slyest creature in all of God's garden.

Bonnie: And one day, he climbed up in a tree in the middle of the garden, a tree that God had told Adam and Eve not to eat from.

George: "S-s-s-so, Eve, did God really s-s-say you shouldn't eat anything in this-s-s garden?"

Bonnie: "Of course not! We can eat the fruit, except that there is this one tree. It's called the Tree of the Knowledge of Good and Evil. We're not supposed to eat fruit from that tree."

George: "But did he s-s-say you couldn't get clos-s-s-se to the fruit?"

Bonnie: "Um. . . no."

George: "Maybe s-s-s-sniff the fruit?"

Bonnie: "Sniffing? Well, no, we can sniff it, I guess, if we want. But we're not supposed to eat it, or even touch it, or else we would die."

George: *(As a storyteller again, to Bonnie)* Did God really say that?

Bonnie: No. God's rule was they couldn't eat it.

George:	So, why'd she say they couldn't touch it?
Bonnie:	She was adding to what God had said. And that was her first mistake.
George:	I thought her first mistake was listening to a talking snake. I mean, Hello, lady! Snakes are not supposed to talk. That should've been your first clue!
Bonnie:	Let's get back to the story.
George:	*(As the tempter again)* "You won't die! Ins-s-s-stead, you'll become more like God. You'll know about what's-s-s-s good and what's-s-s-s evil."
Bonnie:	Eve looked at the tree.
George:	She listened to the snake.
Bonnie:	She reached out her hand and—
George:	Wait a minute!
Bonnie:	What?
George:	What is she doing?
Bonnie:	She's about to eat the fruit!
George:	But why?
Bonnie:	The snake convinced her to. And the fruit looked fresh and sweet and yummy. And she thought it would make her wiser.
George:	But God told her not to!
Bonnie:	Uh-huh.
George:	And she was gonna do it anyway?!
Bonnie:	Uh-huh.
George:	So what about Adam? Where was he during all this?
Bonnie:	He was standing right next to her.
George:	What?! Why didn't he stop her? He heard the whole snake-thing?
Bonnie:	Yeah. Well, he must have been convinced as well.
George:	But—but—but—are you sure?
Bonnie:	Yeah, this is how the story goes.
George:	But—but—
Bonnie:	She reached out her hand, and picked some of the fruit.
George:	*(Dramatically)* Oh, no! I can't watch!
Bonnie:	She lifted it to her mouth—
George:	*(Getting really emotional)* Don't do it, Eve! Don't do it! You're gonna die! Put it back! Stick it on a branch like a Christmas tree ornament or something!
Bonnie:	She opened her mouth—
George:	*(Saying really fast)* And decided not to eat the fruit after all. She put it in a fruit bowl on her dining room table, and lived happily ever after, working as a receptionist in God's front office.
Bonnie:	What?! That's not how it goes!
George:	So she threw it to the ground and said, "I shall not eateth of this fruiteth, for the Lord hath commandedeth me not to eateth of iteth."
Bonnie:	Nope.
George:	But can't we stop her? Isn't there anything we can do?
Bonnie:	Nope. She bit into the fruit, and she liked it so much, she gave some to her husband, Adam. And he—
George:	Put her on a timeout.
Bonnie:	No. He had some, too.

George:	Oh, no! They're gonna die! They're probably gonna choke on it or something. Do they die?
Bonnie:	Nope. Not right away.
George:	But God told them they would, right?
Bonnie:	Yeah. And he always keeps his promises.
George:	But then why didn't they die?
Bonnie:	They do eventually, but because he loved them so much, he let 'em stay alive for a long time. He found a way to both keep his promise and give them a second chance.
George:	Wow. Cool.
Bonnie:	At that moment, when they ate the fruit, they realized they were naked.
George:	*(Throw your arms across your body, as if you were standing there with no clothes on)* AAAAHHHHH! You mean they weren't wearing any clothes?!
Bonnie:	That's right.
George:	Why not?
Bonnie:	Clothes hadn't been invented yet. And neither had bellybuttons.
George:	Huh?
Bonnie:	Never mind. And they felt ashamed of themselves.
George:	No kidding. I'd be ashamed too, if I were walking around naked eating my lunch. *(Remove your hands and stand normal again)*
Bonnie:	The shame came from disobeying God. Before that, they didn't need clothes. So they sewed some fig leaves together for their clothes.
George:	Where'd they get the sewing machine from?
Bonnie:	They didn't use a sewing machine.
George:	Oh. . . . So, a needle pulling thread?
Bonnie:	Right.
George:	Huh. That sounds familiar. *(Singing)* "So, a needle pulling thread. . .."
Bonnie:	And that night, God came looking for them to go for a walk with him in the garden. But they hid from him.
George:	They ran from God.
Bonnie:	Yup.
George:	*(Singing)* "Fa, a long, long way to run!"
Bonnie:	Um. . .
George:	But why did they run?
Bonnie:	Shame. They were still ashamed. Then God called, "Adam! Where are you?"
George:	"Come out, come out, wherever you are!" Wait a minute. God couldn't find 'em?!
Bonnie:	Of course he could. He is God.
George:	Right. . . Well, then why did he call for them? By George, I think I've got it!
Bonnie:	What do you think?
George:	Maybe he was giving them a chance to step out and admit their mistake?
Bonnie:	I think you're right, George. So, finally Adam said, "I was scared when I heard you—"
George:	"Because I thought you were the bogeyman!"
Bonnie:	No, that's not why he was scared! He said, "I was scared because I'm naked!"
George:	*(Act naked again)*
Bonnie:	So they were scared, ashamed, hiding—
George:	And naked.
Bonnie:	Right. And that's how we still feel today when we do something wrong.

George:	We feel naked?
Bonnie:	No. All the other stuff though.
George:	Oh.
Bonnie:	And God said, "Did you eat from the Tree of the Knowledge of Good and Evil?"
George:	*(Acting like Adam)* "Um, yes? But, uh. . . it was all her fault!"
Bonnie:	And God asked Eve, "Is that true?" And she blamed it on the snake, saying it was all his fault.
George:	*(To himself)* Man, a talking snake. I still can't believe she fell for the old talking snake routine. . . .
Bonnie:	God cursed the snake and promised that a child born of a woman would crush the snake, even though he'd be wounded in the process.
George:	Wait a minute! . . . That snake wasn't just any old ordinary snake, was he?
Bonnie:	Nope.
George:	It was really the biggest snake of all in disguise, right?
Bonnie:	The devil?
George:	Yeah.
Bonnie:	You got it. And who crushed the power of the devil?
George:	Jesus!
Bonnie:	Right.
George:	So let me get this straight. They disobeyed God and he gave them a second chance. They still wouldn't admit doing anything wrong and he offered them the promise of a Savior?
Bonnie:	Yup. And he made them new clothes, too.
George:	Good. Because they were naked.
Bonnie:	See? God kept all his promises and was still able to show love.
George:	Wow.
Bonnie:	Then they had to leave the garden.
George:	Why?
Bonnie:	Because of God's love.
George:	What? How does that show love?
Bonnie:	Because if they ate of the Tree of Life, they would live forever under the power of the evil they'd discovered.
George:	Oh.
Bonnie:	But God wanted them to live forever in peace and love instead.
George:	*(Finally getting it)* And the only way he could do that was to let their bodies die so their spirits could live with him forever!
Bonnie:	Right!
George:	And even today, God still offers us forgiveness—
Bonnie:	When we disobey.
George:	*(After a pause)* Wow. They had to leave the garden. I guess you could say they were the first couple ever to eat themselves out of house and home.
Bonnie:	I guess you could.
Together:	The end.

(Bow. Exit.)

Cain Wasn't Abel

3

Based On: Genesis 4

Big Idea: When Cain saw that God didn't approve of his sacrifice, he murdered his brother out of jealousy and rage. We must resist when temptations come into our lives.

Background: Cain repeatedly gave in to his selfish motives and became the world's first murderer. This story shows us how quickly things went downhill after sin entered the world. And yet God's grace can even be seen in this story of rebellion and murder.

Type: Tandem storytelling

Tellers: Bonnie—A serious storyteller trying to tell the story correctly (female or male); George—Her friend, who keeps getting everything mixed up (male or female).

Tools: None

Topics: Anger, consequences, excuses, family relationships, jealousy, rebellion, resentment, self-control, sin, stubbornness, temptation, vengeance

Tips: Both storytellers start onstage, or enter together. Bring up the stage lights, and then begin when the students are quiet.

Script:

Bonnie:	After Adam and Eve had to leave God's garden—
George:	They moved into a condo in the suburbs.
Bonnie:	There were no suburbs.
George:	Oh. A high-rise apartment?
Bonnie:	No, they had a baby boy and they named him—
George:	Alfonso Pasquale!
Bonnie:	No, they named him Cain.
George:	Why didn't they name him Alfonso Pasquale?
Bonnie:	I don't know, they just called him Cain.
George:	Sugar cane.
Bonnie:	No, not sugar cane, just plain Cain. And later on they had another baby. And they named him—
George:	Barney.
Bonnie:	No, Abel.
George:	Abel?
Bonnie:	Right.
George:	They were able to have another baby. They were able to have Abel!
Bonnie:	And Abel watched over the flock of sheep.
George:	I'd watch over the sheep, too.
Bonnie:	Why is that?
George:	I like lamb chops.

Bonnie:	Look. Cain worked out in the fields. Raising crops—
George:	Like sugar cane.
Bonnie:	Well, maybe. . . . But one day, Cain picked some of the fruit he'd grown, and he brought it as an offering to God.
George:	Did Abel bring an offering, too?
Bonnie:	Yes, of sheep.
George:	Lamb chops.
Bonnie:	Right.
George:	Chopped up lambs. Yummy.
Bonnie:	Um, right. Now, God was pleased with—
George:	The lamb chops. By the way, I'm getting hungry.
Bonnie:	God didn't eat the fruit or the lamb chops!
George:	Why not? They smell delicious.
Bonnie:	Look, God was pleased with Abel's offering because he brought his best sheep to God and he brought his offering out of faith—
George:	He believed. . .
Bonnie:	Right.
George:	That the sheep were delicious.
Bonnie:	He believed in God and brought his offering because he loved God. But Cain, well, he didn't please God because—
George:	His plants were all wilty and rotten.
Bonnie:	Well, right. He didn't bring his best to God, nor did he bring his offering out of faith.
George:	He didn't believe.
Bonnie:	Right.
George:	That the fruit was rotten.
Bonnie:	Right—
George:	He knew it was.
Bonnie:	Right. Um. . . And Cain was really mad.
George:	Did he like lamb chops, too?
Bonnie:	No, he was mad because he was jealous of how God favored Abel's offering over his.
George:	Oh. And because he wished his name was Alfonso Pasquale.
Bonnie:	So, the Lord said, "Cain, what's wrong? Why are you so angry? If you do what's right you'll be accepted. But if you do what's wrong, sin is crouching at your door." *(See Genesis 4:7.)*
George:	*(Crouch, look evil)*
Bonnie:	What are you doing?
George:	I'm crouching at his door. *(Growl)*
Bonnie:	". . .Crouching at your door, it desires to control you. But you must master it."
George:	*(Growl again, then stand up normal)* Did he master it?
Bonnie:	Nope. Cain didn't listen to what God told him.
George:	God spoke to him and he ignored it?
Bonnie:	Yup.
George:	That's gonna lead to trouble!
Bonnie:	You're right, it did. Cain invited Abel out into the fields and while they were there, Cain attacked his brother and killed him.
George:	Whoa. Is this where the Lord says, "Where is your brother?"

Bonnie:	Yup. And Cain said, "How should I know? What do I look like? His babysitter?"
George:	But didn't God know what he'd done?
Bonnie:	Well, yeah. But he was giving him a chance to admit what he'd done wrong.
George:	Did he admit it?
Bonnie:	Nope. And God said, "What have you done, Cain?! Your brother's blood has called out to me!"
George:	Talking blood?
Bonnie:	Well, God was using a figure of speech. He meant that Abel's death was calling out for justice.
George:	Ah-ha. What did God say then?
Bonnie:	"Now you're under a curse, Cain." And then, Cain was sent to wander by himself across the world.
George:	Is that the end?
Bonnie:	Pretty much.
George:	*(After a pause)* Man, I wish this story had a happier ending.
Bonnie:	So did Cain. He said, "That's too hard for me! People will be out to get me my whole life!"
George:	Did he say he was sorry?
Bonnie:	No.
George:	Did he ever admit to God what he'd done?
Bonnie:	No.
George:	Did his heart ever change?
Bonnie:	We're not told.
George:	Whoa.
Bonnie:	Then, Adam and Eve had another son and they named this one—
George:	Alfonso Pasquale!
Bonnie:	No, Seth. They named this son Seth. His descendants called on the Lord. But the children of Cain wandered farther and farther from God. Do you know what the lessons of the story are?
George:	Lamb chops go well with sugarcane!
Bonnie:	Nope, wanna try again?
George:	We need to bring our best to God—
Bonnie:	Good.
George:	We should have faith and call on him—
Bonnie:	Right!
George:	We should stay away from sin when it knocks at our door.
Bonnie:	Very good!
George:	And finally—Never name your kids Alfonso Pasquale!
Bonnie:	Oh, brother.
together:	The end.
George:	*(Begin exiting)* Hey, Bonnie, do you know why Cain's offering didn't please God?
Bonnie:	Why, George? Why didn't it please God?
George:	Because Cain wasn't Able.
Bonnie:	He wasn't able.
George:	Right.
Bonnie:	He sure wasn't. . . .

(Fade out the stage lights as the storytellers exit.)

4

The Flood

Based On:	Genesis 6-9
Big Idea:	Even though the world around him was evil, Noah trusted in and obeyed the Lord. As a result, God rescued Noah and his family from destruction.
Background:	As the population of earth grew, great wickedness spread among the people (Genesis 6:5). It broke God's heart to see so much sin in the world. He decided to send a giant flood and wipe out the whole human race. But Noah followed God and had a close relationship with Him. God chose to rescue Noah and his family as well as representatives from the different species of animals and plants from the devastating worldwide flood.
Type:	Tandem storytelling
Tellers:	Dana—A slightly more serious storyteller trying to tell the story correctly (female or male); Matt—Her friend, who occasionally gets things mixed up (male or female).
Tools:	A leafy branch
Topics:	Consequences, faith, following God, God's power, obedience, rebellion, second chances, sin
Tips:	Place the leafy branch in the back of the room before the story begins. Both storytellers start onstage, or enter together. Bring up the stage lights, and then begin when the students are quiet.

Script:

Dana:	Long ago when the earth was young—
Matt:	The people turned away from God.
Dana:	The world was filled with cruel,
Matt:	Mean,
Dana:	Nasty,
Matt:	Rotten,
Dana:	No good,
Matt:	Naughty,
Dana:	Really bad people.
Matt:	But there was one guy who followed the Lord.
Dana:	And his name was Noah.
Matt:	One day, God spoke to Noah and said,
Dana:	"Noah, the world is filled with cruel,
Matt:	Mean,
Dana:	Nasty,
Matt:	Rotten,
Dana:	No good,
Matt:	Naughty,
Dana:	Really bad people.

Matt:	So I've decided to destroy them all.
Dana:	Build a boat big enough for your whole family—
Matt:	*(Quickly)* And two of every kind of animal in the whole wide world."
Dana:	Whoa. That's a big boat.
Matt:	A very big boat.
Dana:	In fact, it was a humongous,
Matt:	Gigantic,
Dana:	Enormous,
Matt:	Gargantuan,
Dana:	Really big boat.
Matt:	So, Noah hammered and sawed and hammered and sawed—
Dana:	And hammered and sawed and hammered and sawed—
Matt:	And hammered and sawed and hammered and sawed—
Dana:	Until—
Matt:	His arm was really tired,
Dana:	And his boat was really done.
Matt:	Then, God told him to get into the boat with his family.
Dana:	And a week later,
Matt:	The rains came down—
Dana:	And the floods came up.
Matt:	And the lifeguards dove in—
Dana:	There were no lifeguards.
Matt:	Then who dove in to save all those people?
Dana:	No one did. The people didn't survive.
Matt:	Oh.
Dana:	And all those cruel,
Matt:	Mean,
Dana:	Nasty,
Matt:	Rotten,
Dana:	No good,
Matt:	Naughty,
Dana:	Really bad people—
Matt:	Were washed away. Whoosh!
Dana:	The sky split open and rains came crashing down.
Matt:	Thunder rolled across the heavens.
Dana:	And even the earth burst open.
Matt:	Waters came from high in the sky,
Dana:	And down in the earth,
Matt:	And the boat rose higher and higher on the waves.
Dana:	And all the people,
Matt:	And all the animals,
Dana:	Were safe inside the humongous,
Matt:	Gigantic,
Dana:	Enormous,

Matt:	Gargantuan,
Dana:	Really big boat.
Matt:	Inside, there were two cows.
Dana:	*(As Matt lists the animals, make the appropriate sound effects)* Moo! Moo!
Matt:	Two snakes.
Dana:	Hiss! Hiss!
Matt:	Two hippos.
Dana:	Blub. Blub.
Matt:	Two worms.
Dana:	Squiggle. Squiggle.
Matt:	Two octopuses.
Dana:	Um—
Matt:	Two sharks.
Dana:	Wait a minute.
Matt:	A couple of eels.
Dana:	No, no, no.
Matt:	And two blue whales.
Dana:	The whales and sharks and eels weren't on the boat, they were in the water!
Matt:	Oh. Eating all the dead people, I guess.
Dana:	That's gross. Look, the rain fell for 40 days—
Matt:	And 40 nights.
Dana:	But Noah,
Matt:	And his wife,
Dana:	And his three sons,
Matt:	And their wives,
Dana:	Were safe and sound inside the humongous,
Matt:	Gigantic,
Dana:	Enormous,
Matt:	Gargantuan,
Dana:	Really big boat.
Matt:	With all those snakes.
Dana:	Hiss! Hiss!
Matt:	Hippos.
Dana:	Blub. Blub.
Matt:	Worms.
Dana:	Squiggle. Squiggle.
Matt:	Octopuses.
Dana:	Isn't that supposed to be octopi?-
Matt:	No thanks, I'm not hungry.
Dana:	Wait a minute.
Matt:	Sharks, eels, and whales—
Dana:	In the water. . . . And, finally, the water covered the whole earth.
Matt:	Even the highest hills and mountains.
Dana:	The water covered the earth for 150 days.

Matt:	That's a long time to be shut up in a boat with a bunch of . . .
Dana:	Oh, no, not again.
Matt:	Cows—
Dana:	Moo! Moo!
Matt:	And snakes.
Dana:	Hiss! Hiss!
Matt:	And hippos.
Dana:	Blub. Blub.
Matt:	And worms.
Dana:	Squiggle. Squiggle.
Matt:	By the way, do you know how Noah kept the milk on the boat from spoiling?
Dana:	Nope. How?
Matt:	He kept it in the cows! . . . And do you know what kind of lights he took on the boat?
Dana:	Nope. What?
Matt:	Floodlights!
Dana:	Oh, brother. . . . Look, we'd better get back to the story.
Matt:	Right! And God remembered Noah and his family and all those animals.
Dana:	And he sent a strong wind.
Matt:	WHOOSH! *(Blow in Dana's face)*
Dana:	*(Cough as if Matt has bad breath)*
Matt:	And the waters began to evaporate—Whoosh!
Dana:	The boat stopped floating and hit the edge of Mount Ararat.
Matt:	Mount Acrobat?
Dana:	No, Ararat. And then, after many days, Noah opened the door and sent out a dove.
Matt:	*(Flap your arms like wings)*
Dana:	It was a rather big dove. . . . *(Matt flies around the audience, and comes back on stage)* . . . But the dove could find no place to land, because the water was still too high. Noah reached out his arm, and the dove landed on it.
Matt:	*(Look at Dana's arm, then at the audience, and try to jump on her arm)*
Dana:	A week later, he sent out the dove again.
Matt:	*(Flap your arms like wings and fly around the audience again)*
Dana:	Toward evening, he returned with an olive branch in his beak.
Matt:	*(Grab the leafy branch from the back of the room and carry it up in your hand)*
Dana:	Um, I said "in his beak," not "in his wing."
Matt:	*(Stick it in your mouth and keep flapping your arms in front of the audience)*
Dana:	A week later, he sent out the dove again.
Matt:	*(Fly off again)*
Dana:	This time, the dove did not return.
Matt:	*(Go out the door, out of the room)*
Dana:	*(Yelling)* But the storyteller did return!
Matt:	*(Open the door, peek your head in)* Oh, okay. *(Come back onstage)*
Dana:	Finally, twelve and a half months after the flood began, Noah and his family left the boat and brought with them all of those cows—
Matt:	*(Don't do anything)*
Dana:	What are you waiting for?

Matt:	I don't do the animal sounds. That's your part.
Dana:	Oh, c'mon, please?
Matt:	*(Shake your head "no")*
Dana:	*(Sighing)* Oh, alright.
Matt:	The cows!
Dana:	*(Make all the animal sounds reluctantly)* Moo. Moo.
Matt:	And snakes.
Dana:	Hiss. Hiss.
Matt:	And hippos.
Dana:	Blub. Blub.
Matt:	And worms.
Dana:	Squiggle. Squiggle.
Matt:	And the rest of the animals.
Dana:	Noah and his family worshipped God,
Matt:	And God promised never again to send a flood across the whole world.
Dana:	God sealed his promise with a rainbow,
Matt:	And blessed Noah and his family,
Dana:	And sent them out into the fresh, clean world. Away from that humongous,
Matt:	Gigantic,
Dana:	Enormous,
Matt:	Gargantuan,
Dana:	Really big boat.
Together:	The end. *(Bow)*
Matt:	*(Begin to exit)* With all those—
Dana:	Nope. I'm not gonna do it.
Matt:	C'mon, c'mon. Cows! Go on!
Dana:	Moo. Moo. . .

(Fade out the stage lights.)

The Master of Disasters

9

Based On:	Exodus 5–12
Big Idea:	God delivered his people from slavery into freedom.
Background:	When the king of Egypt refused to let God's people go, God sent a series of disasters on the land, bringing glory to himself and freedom to his people.
Type:	Version #1—Storymime with audience participation Version #2—Tandem monologues
Tellers:	For the storymime version, one person reads or tells the story while the other person leads the actions. The students then copy the actions. For the tandem monologues version, two storytellers share the story of the crossing of the Red Sea from the perspective of an Israelite (male or female) and an Egyptian Soldier (male, or perhaps female).
Tools:	None
Topics:	Consequences, courage, freedom, God's power, listening, obedience, Passover, prophecy fulfillment, second chances, stubbornness
Tips:	For the storymime version, it might be helpful if the person doing the actions has some experience in mime, theater, or just likes acting goofy. The storytellers could be either men or women. The tandem monologues version is a little more intense and will work better for children in upper elementary grades. For both versions, the storytellers both start onstage, or enter together. Bring up the stage lights, and then begin when the students are quiet.

The Master of Disasters (storymime version)

What to say:	What to do:
Moses and Aaron went before the king.	*Bow down with hands stretched out.*
They said, "Let God's people go!"	*Point off into the distance.*
But the king just laughed.	*Slap your leg and laugh.*
"Who is this God? Why should I listen to him?"	*Fold arms, look stern.*
"Get out of here and get back to work."	*Shoo them off with your hands.*
Then, he had the slave drivers whip the Israelites.	*Pretend that you are using a whip.*
Moses prayed to God.	*Fold hands, look up reverently.*
And he told the Israelites of God's power.	*Flex muscles.*
But they wouldn't believe, because they were too discouraged.	*Look down, sigh, and shake your head.*
So Moses and Aaron returned to the king.	*Bow down with hands stretched out.*
To prove God's power, Aaron threw down his stick.	*Pretend to throw down a stick.*

And it turned into a snake.	*Look snaky and act slithery.*
The king's magicians threw down their sticks.	*Pretend to throw down more sticks.*
They also turned into snakes.	*Look snaky and act slithery.*
But Aaron's snake ate their snakes.	*Pretend to swallow, smile, and rub your tummy.*
But still, the king wouldn't let God's people go.	*Put your hands on your hips, shake your head "no."*
Then Moses and Aaron turned the river water into blood—	*Make a disgusted face.*
And the river stank.	*Hold your nose.*
But the king wouldn't let God's people go.	*Put your hands on your hips, shake your head "no."*
Then God sent frogs,	*Hop like a frog.*
And flies,	*Buzz like a fly.*
Sick cows,	*Hold your stomach and look like you're going to throw up.*
And big ugly blisters. . . that really itched.	*Scratch yourself and look sore.*
Then God sent hail.	*Put your hands up to cover your head.*
With lots of lightning;	*Pretend that your finger is lightning and strike the person next to you.*
It even knocked down the trees.	*Take one arm and tip it over like a falling tree. Yell,* **"Timber!"**
And each time Moses stopped the plagues. . .	*Put your hand out like you're a police officer stopping traffic.*
When the king asked him to.	*Fold your hands and pretend to plead.*
But still the king wouldn't let God's people go.	*Put your hands on your hips, shake your head "no."*
Then, God sent grasshoppers that hopped all over the place,	*Go crazy, hopping all over.*
And even chewed up all the crops.	*Pretend to chew on corn on the cob.*
Then God sent a wind that blew the locusts away.	*Blow really hard at the person next to you.*
Then, God sent darkness.	*Close your eyes and feel around like you're standing in the dark.*
But still, the king wouldn't let God's people go.	*Put your hands on your hips, shake your head "no."*
Finally, God said, "There will be one more disaster."	*Hold one finger up high in the air.*

"Tell the Israelites to paint their doorframes—	*Pretend to dip a paintbrush and paint a doorframe.*
With the blood of a lamb."	*Make sheep ears on your head with your hands and say "baa."*
And so that night, while the Egyptians were asleep. . .	*Put your head against your hands, pretending to sleep.*
God sent his mighty angel. . .	*Draw a sword and hold it in front of you.*
Who killed the firstborn Egyptians.	*Swing your sword around and poke it forward.*
Every house in Egypt was filled with sad people.	*Make a sad face and pretend to cry.*
But the Israelites slept safe and sound.	*Put your head against your hands, pretending to sleep.*
Finally, the king said, "Get out of here! I never want to see any of you again!"	*Point off into the distance.*
As the Israelites left, the Egyptians gave them their gold. . .	*Pretend to bounce a bag of gold coins in your hand.*
Their fancy earrings. . .	*Grab your earlobe and show it off to the person next to you.*
And their clothes.	*Put your hands in front of you and cover yourself as if you have no clothes.*
And God led them through the desert. . .	*Pretend to wipe sweat from your brow.*
Just as he had promised Moses at the burning bush.	*Hold out your hands in front of you and warm them as if you were in front of a campfire.*
The end.	*Bow and take a seat.*

The Master of Disasters (tandem monologues version)

Israelite: For nearly 400 years we'd been their slaves. But then, Moses and Aaron arrived promising that God would deliver us. That's when the plagues started.

Egyptian: The Israelites had been nothing but trouble for a long time. They claimed that their God was causing all the plagues. We just kept telling ourselves they were natural disasters and strange coincidences.

Israelite: Moses said this would be the last one. The last plague. But it would also be the worst one of all.

Egyptian: Their God couldn't really be in control. We weren't afraid of him and we weren't afraid of them.

Israelite: Moses explained that if we prepared a special meal and killed a lamb and put its blood on our doorframes, we would be saved.

Egyptian: We heard rumors about it. At twilight the Israelites were all out there, killing their lambs and roasting their suppers.

Israelite: We ate the Lord's Passover and then we waited.

Egyptian: We closed our doors and then we waited.

Israelite: Just after midnight we heard the sounds of screams echoing through the streets.

Egyptian: Just after midnight, I went in to check on my son.

Israelite: It was just as the Lord had said.

Egyptian: No. . . No. . . It can't be!

Israelite: God was striking dead the firstborn sons of all the Egyptians.

Egyptian: My son was. . . my son was. . . dead. . .

Israelite: God was in control. And he was on our side.

Egyptian: In all the history of Egypt, there has never been a night of so much sadness and crying as that night.

Israelite: Of course we were sad that the Egyptians had brought this on themselves by rejecting God. But we were also a little happy because we knew that our long years in slavery were finally over.

Egyptian: We wanted them gone. Once and for all. Their God was too powerful.

Israelite: Our God had rescued us. We were finally free!

(Freeze. Fade out the stage lights. Exit.)

The Giant Match-up

Based On: 1 Samuel 17

Big Idea: With God's help, David killed Goliath and became one of Israel's greatest heroes.

Background: God's people, the Israelites, were embroiled in conflict with the ruthless Philistines. Saul, the king of Israel, was beginning to show cowardice as a leader. When no one else stepped up to face Goliath, a young man with great faith in God came forward and became Israel's greatest hero.

Type: Sports Announcer

Tellers: Bo and Gary are TV sports announcers giving the play-by-play of David's victory over Goliath. Bo is somewhat clueless (yet a bit of a "know-it-all"). Gary has more of the right answers.

Tools: Papers, clipboards, microphones, and other sports announcer paraphernalia

Topics: Bullies, conviction, courage, faith, giftedness, God's power, success

Tips: Have fun pretending to be sports announcers during this story. You may wish to dress the part with old suit coats and microphones. Whenever Bo says, "That's right. I do!" he does it very dramatically. Both storytellers start onstage, or enter together. Bring up the stage lights, and then begin when the students are quiet.

Script:

Bo: Well, Gary, we're here at the scene of the battle today. And, as you know, it promises to be a great fight!

Gary: It sure does, Bo. On the one side we've got Goliath. He measures in at—you're not gonna believe this—

Bo: Try me.

Gary: Over 9 feet tall!

Bo: I don't believe it.

Gary: I knew you wouldn't. And he's looking for a fight, but no one seems to be stepping up to the plate to face the challenge.

Bo: Well, you know what they say, "The bigger they are, the harder the are to feed."

Gary: Um, I think you mean, "The bigger they are, the harder they fall."

Bo: That's right, Gary. I do! But wait! What's this? There's a kid running out onto the playing field! *(To audience)* Hey, kid! Come back here! *(To Gary)* Some momma is not gonna be happy today.

Gary: Um. . . That's not a lost boy, Bo. That's the guy who's gonna fight the giant.

Bo: Yeah right. That's a good one there, Gary. You crack me up.

Gary: *(Whispering)* I'm not kidding.

Bo: You're not kidding? Whew. In that case, it's kinda like David going up against Goliath out there today.

Gary: Bo, it is David going up against Goliath out there today.

Bo: That's right, Gary. It is! Well, let's see what happens. *(Shuffling through papers)* We don't have too many stats on this kid. He must have just moved up from the minors.

Gary: *(Reading from a stat sheet)* It says here, he was a shepherd.

Bo:	I've never heard of that team before—
Gary:	It isn't a team, Bo. I mean, the boy watched over the sheep. And, he's a songwriter!
Bo:	So he's more qualified to take care of the mascot or sing the national anthem than to face this giant. . .
Gary:	Well, he once killed a lion and a bear with his bare hands. . .
Bo:	And look at this! He has red hair! Let's hope that helps him.
Gary:	*(Pause for a moment, look at Bo as if to say, "What are you talking about?" Then point in the distance)* There he goes! He has a stick and a slingshot.
Bo:	That's it?! I don't believe it! That giant has an industrial strength Kevlar bulletproof vest! Reinforced airline steel shield! A spear as big as a Patriot missile—
Gary:	Wait a minute. . . Listen. . . We've got audio from Goliath's headset microphone. *(Cover your mouth and speak for Goliath)* "Ha! What do I look like? A dog? That you want me to fetch your sticks!"
Bo:	He's talking trash!
Gary:	He sure is, Bo.
Bo:	Wait, I believe we're getting a live satellite feed on David. . . *(Cover your mouth and speak for David).* "We don't need no stinking weapons! The Lord is on our side!" *(Shuffle papers, look for info)* Hmm. . . . The Lord. . . Hmm. . . . Let's see. . . I don't see him on the roster. . . .
Gary:	There goes the giant and his shield-holder. They're moving in fast!
Bo:	And what's this! There goes the boy. He's running in toward the giant! I repeat, he's running in toward the giant!
Gary:	You know, Bo, David's showing some good speed out there today.
Bo:	He sure is, Gary!
Gary:	He's reaching into his shepherd's bag! Nice form!
Bo:	He's got a stone. I repeat, he's got a stone!
Gary:	The giant is raising his spear. Bo, all the eyes in this arena are glued to David and that giant.
Bo:	That's right, Gary. They are! And boy do they look silly with all those eyes glued to them.
Gary:	That's not what I meant. Look, David is swinging the stone over his head!
Bo:	We'll be right back after a short commercial beak. *(Freeze for a moment, and then talk informally to each other. If you choose, insert local names, jokes, or references your students will identify with. Hold your finger to your ear as if checking a microphone)* Oh, wait. We're back on the air. . .
Gary:	*(Addressing the audience)* David is swinging the stone over his head!
Bo:	Goliath doesn't seem phased at all by this, Gary. He's still moving toward the kid.
Gary:	The stone is released—
Bo:	It's a fast ball—
Gary:	We're clocking it at 107 miles per hour!
Bo:	There's only a handful of people in the world who can sling a rock at speeds like that.
Gary:	That kid from Bethlehem has got some arm!
Bo:	That's right, Gary. He does!
Gary:	And Goliath seems to think he can best deflect that stone by using his forehead.
Bo:	I would have used my shield in a situation like that, Gary.
Gary:	Me, too, Bo. But let's see what happens. This giant's got lots of battle experience—Let's see. . . *(Looking over papers as if checking statistics)* he was drafted as a kid and has been in the pros for nearly 20 years. And he's never lost a match.
Bo:	Oh! What's this! The stone has sunk into the giant's forehead. I repeat, the stone has sunk into the giant's forehead!
Gary:	It's lodged in there, oh, about 5 or 6 inches.
Bo:	You know, Gary, that's gotta hurt!

24 Tandem Bible Story Scripts for Children's Ministry

Gary:	Yeah, he's gonna feel that one in the morning.
Bo:	That's what I call using your head.
Gary:	He's on his way down.
Bo:	He's falling. . .
Gary:	Falling. . .
Bo:	Falling. . .

(Both storytellers bump off their seats as the giant hits the ground)

Gary:	Yikes!
Bo:	The giant has hit the ground!
Gary:	And here comes David. He's running toward the giant.
Bo:	What's he gonna do, Gary? Maybe a little end-zone dance?
Gary:	I don't know, Bo. . . Nope, look at that. He's got the giant's sword in his hand.
Bo:	Good game plan. He didn't bring his own sword so he's gonna use the giant's sword instead!
Gary:	Brilliant strategy!
Bo:	Oh, look at that. He's slicing off the head of the giant. I repeat, he's slicing off the head of the giant!
Gary:	You know, Bo, anytime you get your head sliced off like that, it really takes the fight out of you.
Bo:	It sure does, Gary.
Gary:	And there go the Philistines.
Bo:	Check out the look in their eyes!
Gary:	Yup. It looks to me like they're either terrified or they've got to go to the bathroom really bad.
Bo:	So, the Philistines are taking off.
Gary:	And here come the Israelites!
Bo:	The race is on!
Gary:	And it looks like—yes! Yes! The Philistines are getting kicked all over the field!
Bo:	Yikes. It's not looking good for them here today. They're getting cut down left and right by the Israelites. I repeat, *(motion for the audience to join you as you say this)* they're getting cut down left and right by the Israelites!
Gary:	It looks like David and his God were victorious out there today!
Bo:	It sure does, Gary.
Gary:	And it looks like David is gonna keep the giant's head as a souvenir.
Bo:	Ew. . . I hope he's not gonna mount it on the wall above his fireplace.
Gary:	I don't think he will, Bo.
Bo:	Why not?
Gary:	His tent doesn't have a fireplace.
Bo:	Oh, yeah. . . . Well, Goliath sure got deheaded and befeated out there today.
Gary:	Um, you mean, beheaded and defeated.
Bo:	That's right, Gary. I do!
Gary:	And that's our game for today! Join us next time for more live coverage!
Bo:	Until then, this is Bo Donut—
Gary:	And Gary Gumball, signing off!

(Freeze. Fade out the stage lights. Exit.)

Unidentified Flying Angels

Based On: Luke 2:1-20

Big Idea: God sent his Son into the world to become our Savior.

Background: When Jesus was born, the first people who found out about it (besides Mary and Joseph!) were the shepherds watching over their flocks of sheep. The shepherds quickly spread the news about Jesus' birth and everyone who heard it was impressed and amazed (Luke 2:20). The promised Messiah had finally arrived.

Type: Interview

Tellers: Biff—A shepherd on his way to worship the baby Jesus (male or female); Les Braincell—A corny detective investigating strange lights over Bethlehem (male).

Tools: A trench coat, notepad, and magnifying glass for Les

Topics: Angels, Christmas, God's love, hope, Jesus, listening, prophecy fulfillment, witnessing, worship

Tips: Les Braincell's character is meant to be corny, so ham it up, be goofy, exaggerated, and silly. Since he appears in several sketches, you may wish to use a costume that he could wear whenever he tells one of these stories. Les starts the scene onstage. Bring up the stage lights, and then begin when the students are quiet.

Script:

Les: I'm Les, Les Braincell here, the world's greatest detective dude. I'm on the scene here in Bethlehem, where strange lights have been seen in the night sky. *(Pull out a magnifying glass and look through it. As Biff enters, look at him and yell)* Aha! Are you a clue?

Biff: Nope. I'm a shepherd.

Les: A shepherd, huh?

Biff: Yes.

Les: Then you're an expert on sheep?

Biff: Of course.

Les: You know all about lambs?

Biff: Yes, I do.

Les: Then what did Mary have?

Biff: A little baby.

Les: No! A little lamb! Whose fleece was white as. . .

Biff: Swaddling clothes?

Les: No! Snow! And everywhere that Mary went. . .

Biff: Um, Mary hasn't gone anywhere. She's still in the stable.

Les: She's on the table? Is it suppertime?

Biff: No. She's in the stable.

Les: She's unstable! Don't worry, I'll protect you! I'm an expert in four types of martial arts. *(Scream loudly and do various karate moves.)*

Biff:	Mary is in the stable with Joseph.
Les:	*(Singing to the tune of "Someone's in the Kitchen With Dinah")* Mary's in the stable with Joseph, Mary's in the stable, I know-oh-oh-oh. Mary's in the stable with Joseph, strummin' on the old banjo!
Biff:	Um, she's not strummin' on the old banjo.
Les:	Tuba?
Biff:	Listen. Mary is in the stable and had a baby tonight. She just got here from out of town.
Les:	Aha! Where's she from?
Biff:	Um, she's from Nazareth.
Les:	*(Looking up at the sky)* And what solar system is that in?
Biff:	Ours.
Les:	Aha! An undiscovered planet.
Biff:	It's just down the road from here.
Les:	The planet? Another planet has landed on the road? Watch out! Meteor shower!
Biff:	It's a town. The town of Nazareth. That's where she lives with her fiancée.
Les:	*(Suspiciously)* But yet, they've come here tonight to have their baby, singing "fee-fi-fiddle-ee-i-o." Something fishy is going on.
Biff:	*(Looking at Les)* You could say that again.
Les:	*(Beginning to repeat himself)* But yet, they've come here tonight to have their baby, singing "fee-fi-fiddle"—
Biff:	Not the whole thing. Look, I'm going to visit them right now. Do you wanna come along?
Les:	I can't. I'm on duty. Looking for clues about why there were strange lights in the sky. I think it has something to do with that planet you were telling me about.
Biff:	Maybe it was the angels.
Les:	Are they playing here tonight? Who's the game against, the Yankees?
Biff:	There were angels in the sky.
Les:	*(Intensely)* Angels in the sky? Are you serious? Don't play games with me here, man! Where's the proof? Where's the evidence? Where's the DNA?
Biff:	Angels don't have DNA.
Les:	Oh. Then how do you know it was angels and not aliens?
Biff:	Believe me, when you see one, you can tell.
Les:	By their uniforms?
Biff:	Something like that. . . We were in the field watching over our sheep.
Les:	Aha! There you go again, impersonating a shepherd.
Biff:	I am a shepherd.
Les:	*(Thoughtfully)* Then I must be impersonating someone. Maybe a private eye. Maybe I'm not who I say I am. Maybe I'm really Tom Cruise *(or another movie star or popular sports celebrity)* in disguise.
Biff:	I doubt it.
Les:	Okay. So what did the angels say?
Biff:	They said our Savior has been born tonight in the city of Bethlehem.
Les:	Aha!
Biff:	Aha what? Why did you say "aha?"
Les:	No reason. I just like saying, "Aha!"
Biff:	Oh. And then the angels praised God and sang a song.
Les:	Of sixpence? A pocketful of rye? Four and twenty blackbirds baked in a pie?

Biff:	No, a song of praise about God. And the baby who was born.
Les:	Aha! Were the angels riding in UFOs?
Biff:	Uh, I don't think so. There was also this star some of the guys noticed.
Les:	A star? A star? Shining in the night? *(Singing these next lines to the tune of "Do You Hear What I Hear?")* Or it could be somebody's kite! Or, it could be somebody's kite!
Biff:	It was a star. Trust me.
Les:	That's very unusual. A star in the night sky?!
Biff:	There are thousands of stars shining in the night.
Les:	Since when?
Biff:	Um, creation.
Les:	Oh. Well, that explains a lot.
Biff:	So do you want to come with me or not?
Les:	*(Accusingly)* Yes, I do. What do you have to say about that? *(They begin to exit)*
Biff:	Um, try not to scare the baby, okay?

(Begin to exit. Begin to fade out the sage lights.)

Les:	Aha!
Biff:	You can stop that now.
Les:	Okay. I will. *(Look through magnifying glass at the students)* Aha! More clues!
Biff:	Those aren't clues.
Les:	Are you saying I'm clueless?
Biff:	You said it not me. . . .

The Missing Mini-Messiah

Based On: Luke 2:41-52

Big Idea: Even from an early age Jesus put God's kingdom and God's priorities first.

Background: We don't know much about Jesus' childhood. Luke tells us the only story about Jesus as a young man. When Jesus was 12 years old, his mother and step-father took him to the temple to celebrate the Jewish Passover. But when his family left without him, Jesus stayed behind learning about and teaching God's word.

Type: Interview

Tellers: Mary—the mother of Jesus who lost track of him when she left for home after a busy week in Jerusalem (female); Les Braincell—A corny detective investigating rumors of a missing boy (male).

Tools: A trench coat, notepad, and magnifying glass for Les

Topics: Family relationships, following God, God's Word, Jesus, priorities, purpose

Tips: Les Braincell's character is meant to be corny, so ham it up, be goofy, exaggerated, and silly. Since he appears in several sketches, you may wish to use a costume that he could wear whenever he tells one of these stories. Both storytellers start onstage, or enter together. Bring up the stage lights, and then begin when the students are quiet.

Script

Les: I'm Les, Les Braincell here, the world's greatest detective dude. I'm on the scene here in Jerusalem interviewing Mary—Um, what did you say your last name is?

Mary: I didn't.

Les: Alright, Mrs. Ididnt.

Mary: No, I mean I didn't tell you my last name.

Les: Aha! So you want me to guess it, huh? Smith?. . . No, Dingleheimer. . . Wait, wait, I'll get it. . . Mary, Mary Quitecontraryhowdoesyourgardengrow! That's it!

Mary: I don't have a last name.

Les: And why not? Are you in disguise? Incognito? Are you the victim of identity theft?!

Mary: Last names haven't been invented yet.

Les: Oh.

Mary: Most people just call me Mary, the mother of Jesus; or Mary, the wife of Joseph. Some people call me Mary, full of grace.

Les: Okay, Mary the mother of Joseph, can you tell us what happened here today.

Mary: I'm the mother of Jesus. And it was actually the other day. We were here in Jerusalem.

Les: Who is we? You and who makes we?

Mary: No, that makes three.

Les: Oh.

Mary: My husband and I and our son, Jesus.

Les:	Aha! Just as I suspected! It's all coming together!
Mary:	What's coming together?
Les:	I have no idea.
Mary:	Oh.
Les:	So, you have a son!
Mary:	Of course I have a son. That's why they call me the mother of Jesus.
Les:	Oh. That's what I thought! So what happened to the boy?
Mary:	Well, he disappeared!
Les:	Aha! So, he's a magician!
Mary:	No, he's not a magician. But the boy just disappeared.
Les:	Whose boy?
Mary:	My boy.
Les:	Your boy!
Mary:	*(Shaking your head)* Oh, boy!
Les:	Your son!
Mary:	My son.
Les:	Whose son?
Mary:	God's son.
Les:	I thought you said it was your son?
Mary:	I did.
Les:	Are you claiming to be God!?
Mary:	No, look, it's a long story. He's both my son and God's son, but I'm not God. I'm just Mary.
Les:	The mother of Jesus—
Mary:	Right.
Les:	So what happened then? Did you call 911 on your cell phone?
Mary:	No.
Les:	Did you contact the FBI?
Mary:	Um, no.
Les:	Hire a private detective? Radio for help? Bring in the crime lab?
Mary:	No—
Les:	*(Getting carried away, shaking her)* Why not, woman! What's wrong with you? This is your son we're talking about here! Your son goes missing and you don't even call the police?! What kind of a mother are you? Answer me!
Mary:	But, none of that stuff has been invented yet.
Les:	It hasn't?
Mary:	Nope. Police don't exist and neither do the FBI, crime labs, or cell phones.
Les:	Where do you live?
Mary:	The question isn't where, it's when.
Les:	Okay, when do you live? What year is it?
Mary:	12.
Les:	Twelve what?
Mary:	Just 12.
Les:	You're saying it's 12 o'clock?
Mary:	No, it's 12. Just plain 12.

Les:	Midnight.
Mary:	It's 12.
Les:	Oh, you mean like it's the year 1200. It's the middle ages or something?
Mary:	No. We haven't made it to the middle ages yet. It's still the early ages. The year is 12 A.D.
Les:	Aha! So Jesus is 12 years old?
Mary:	That's right.
Les:	Why didn't you say so?
Mary:	I did.
Les:	Oh. He's almost a teenager?
Mary:	What's a teenager?
Les:	You've got a lot to learn there, Mary. Look, when he went missing, what did you do?
Mary:	We looked for my son. We looked all over for him.
Les:	Did you check with mall security?
Mary:	No.
Les:	Did you look in the parking lot?
Mary:	What's a parking lot? Look, we searched with all our relatives. We thought maybe he was with someone else in their—
Les:	Minivan.
Mary:	No, caravan.
Les:	Caravan?
Mary:	Yeah.
Les:	Dodge or Plymouth?
Mary:	Camel.
Les:	I don't think I've heard of that manufacturer. . . So what did you do then?
Mary:	We went back to Jerusalem to look.
Les:	Was he kidnapped? Wait—God-napped?
Mary:	Nope.
Les:	Abducted by pirates?
Mary:	Nope.
Les:	*(Getting carried away again)* Was he at Six Flags? A movie theater? A sleepover? How'd you find him, by surfing the web? Where was he? Don't keep me in suspense any longer! Tell me! I can't take it anymore! Ah!
Mary:	Are you okay?
Les:	No, I'm Les. Les Braincell, the world's greatest detective dude. Who are you?
Mary:	Most people just call me Mary, the mother of—wait a minute. We went through this already.
Les:	Just testing you.
Mary:	Oh, well, anyway, my son was at church.
Les:	What?!
Mary:	At church.
Les:	Your kid was at church for three days?
Mary:	Uh-huh.
Les:	Was it like a lock-in or something?
Mary:	No.
Les:	What did you do? Sign a parental release form and take him home?

Mary:	Well, I got kind of angry. I said, "What do you think you're doing here? We've been looking all over for you!"
Les:	Aha! And what did he say?
Mary:	Well, he said, "Why were you looking for me? Didn't you know that I'd have to be here, in my Father's house?"
Les:	His father lived in the church? What, was he the janitor?
Mary:	His Father is God.
Les:	Oh, yeah. Right.
Mary:	Well, we didn't really understand what he meant. I mean, I knew he was a special child sent from God. But it took me most of my life to really understand what all that meant.
Les:	Well, did you get in trouble with the department of health and human services? Did you get accused of neglect? Did he have to go live in a foster family? Don't leave us in suspense, woman!
Mary:	Um, he just came back home with us—back to Nazareth.
Les:	Nazareth, huh? I think I've heard of that before. . . .
Mary:	And he was always obedient to us. And he grew smarter and stronger and friendlier and closer to God every day.
Les:	Well, I guess that about wraps up this case. . . . Jesus is no longer missing! So, where is Jesus now?
Mary:	Um, it's a long story. . . . C'mon, I'll fill you in. . . .

(As the storytellers exit, fade out the stage lights.)

The Baptism of Jesus

Based On: Matthew 3 and Luke 3:1-22

Big Idea: God was pleased with Jesus for being baptized and fulfilling all righteousness. God is pleased when we admit our sins and are baptized as well.

Background: John the Baptist was preparing the way for Jesus by preaching to the people and baptizing them when they admitted their sins and committed to live for God. Before beginning his preaching ministry, Jesus was baptized by John in the Jordan River.

Type: Tandem storytelling

Tellers: Bonnie—A serious storyteller trying to tell the story correctly (female or male); George—Her friend, who keeps getting everything mixed up (male or female).

Tools: None

Topics: Baptism, conversion, following God, Holy Spirit, Jesus, ministry, new life, obedience, repentance

Tips: Different churches have different views about the timing and role of baptism in the life of believers, so use discernment in teaching about baptism. Both storytellers start onstage, or enter together. Bring up the stage lights, and then begin when the students are quiet.

Script

Bonnie: Jesus had a cousin named John.

George: But everyone called him John the Baptist because he went around baptizing people by dunking them under the water.

Bonnie: Hey, George, do you know what John the Baptist and Winnie the Pooh have in common?

George: Um. What?

Bonnie: They both have the same middle name—"The." Get it? John the Baptist and Winnie the Pooh

George: I get it. I get it.

Bonnie: Now, the Bible says John's baptism was one of repentance—

George: Did you say, "a rip in his pants?"

Bonnie: No, repentance.

George: What's that?

Bonnie: That's a change of heart toward God.

George: That's better than a rip in your pants.

Bonnie: It sure is.

George: So, they felt sorry for something bad they'd done?

Bonnie: Yeah. And they wanted God to forgive them.

George: Okay.

Bonnie: And this was a way of saying they were depending on God.

George: I get it. And God would forgive their sins.

Bonnie:	Right.
George:	And buy 'em a new pair of pants.
Bonnie:	Wrong. But, as the people came, John would tell them about God's plan for their lives.
George:	Mostly he was there to prepare them to hear the message of Jesus.
Bonnie:	Right. So then Jesus walked up and asked John to baptize him.
George:	What?!
Bonnie:	Jesus asked John to baptize him.
George:	But you said John baptized people who'd done things wrong—
Bonnie:	Right.
George:	Right?
Bonnie:	Right.
George:	Who'd done things right?
Bonnie:	No, wrong.
George:	Who'd done wrong things?
Bonnie:	Right.
George:	I'm right that they're wrong?
Bonnie:	Right.
George:	And they wanted to right their wrongs, right?
Bonnie:	Right.
George:	But Jesus wasn't wrong!
Bonnie:	Right.
George:	He had done no wrong.
Bonnie:	That's right.
George:	I don't even know what I'm talking about anymore!
Bonnie:	John baptized those who'd done wrong.
George:	But he baptized Jesus!
Bonnie:	Right.
George:	Are you saying Jesus did wrong stuff?!
Bonnie:	No. That's why when Jesus asked John to baptize him, John was like, "What?! You oughtta baptize me! You don't need to do this! I'm the one who does!"
George:	So John refused?
Bonnie:	Right.
George:	What'd Jesus say then?
Bonnie:	Jesus said, "Let's do it. It's the right thing to do."
George:	I'm not sure I get it.
Bonnie:	Jesus wanted to do everything right. Right?
George:	Right.
Bonnie:	And nothing wrong.
George:	Right.
Bonnie:	To fulfill everything that was right even though he never did anything wrong!
George:	Okay. Whatever you say.
Bonnie:	So, John went and baptized Jesus.
George:	Because it was right?
Bonnie:	Right.

George:	I'm still not sure I understand why Jesus was baptized. . .
Bonnie:	Well, some people think he wanted to identify with sinners. . . Others say it was an example for us to get baptized, too. . . But either way, we know it pleased God, the Father.
George:	How do we know that?
Bonnie:	Well, because when Jesus came up out of the water the sky opened up.
George:	Uh-oh.
Bonnie:	Why, uh-oh?
George:	Thunderstorm.
Bonnie:	There was no thunderstorm.
George:	Blizzard?
Bonnie:	No, it was like the door to heaven opened up—
George:	Like a trapdoor?
Bonnie:	Well, I guess so.
George:	Did anyone fall out?
Bonnie:	No, but the Spirit of God floated down—
George:	Ah!
Bonnie:	What?
George:	He's gonna squish me.
Bonnie:	Jesus wasn't afraid the Spirit was gonna squish him. The Spirit was in the form of a dove. And it landed on his shoulder.
George:	Uh-oh.
Bonnie:	What?
George:	You know what doves do when they land on your shoulder.
Bonnie:	Look, it wasn't that kind of dove.
George:	It was the dove of love.
Bonnie:	Well, right. And the voice from heaven said—
George:	"Don't make me come down there!"
Bonnie:	No, he said—
George:	"Has anyone seen my dove, someone left the door open up here!"
Bonnie:	No. He said, "That's my son, whom I love a whole, whole lot and I'm very happy with him!"
George:	Cool!
Bonnie:	Yeah, so you see, it pleased God that Jesus did everything right.
George:	Even getting baptized.
Bonnie:	Right.
George:	Even though he'd never done anything wrong?
Bonnie:	Right.
George:	He was all right.
Bonnie:	Right.
George:	He was downright, upright, outright alright.
Bonnie:	That's right.
Together:	The end.

(Fade out the stage lights as the storytellers exit.)

No Dessert in the Desert

14

Based On: Mark 1:12-13 and Luke 4:1-13

Big Idea: Jesus withstood Satan's temptations by turning to God's word. We can learn from Jesus' example to turn to God's word whenever we're tempted today.

Background: Immediately after Jesus' baptism, the Holy Spirit led him into the desert to be tempted by the devil. Despite Satan's persistence, Jesus never once gave in to sin.

Type: Narralogue

Tellers: Narrator—a storyteller who tells the story of Jesus' temptation (male or female); Angel—a storyteller who tells the story from the angel's perspective (male or female).

Tools: None; or you may wish to have the Angel dress in a white shirt, dress, or robe

Topics: Angels, choices, conviction, demons, following God, God's Word, Jesus, obedience, priorities, self-control, temptation

Tips: This story is based on the account found in Luke 4:1-13. Matthew records the devil's temptations in a slightly different order (see Matthew 4:1-11). Both storytellers start onstage, or enter together. Bring up the stage lights, and then begin when the students are quiet.

Script:

Narrator: After Jesus was baptized in the Jordan River, the Holy Spirit led him into the wilderness.

Angel: I was there. I saw it all. God had sent several of us angels to be with Jesus out there in the desert to help him and comfort him.

Narrator: Jesus had nothing to eat for nearly six weeks, and boy was he hungry.

Angel: I could hear his stomach growling. I don't know what it's like to be hungry, but it doesn't sound like a whole lot of fun.

Narrator: All during the forty days the devil tempted Jesus—

Angel: I don't know how Jesus managed. I just don't know how he did it. No human could ever last that long without giving in. No one ever had before, no one ever has since.

Narrator: The devil approached Jesus and said, "If you really are who you claim to be, the Son of God, then turn these stones into a loaf of whole wheat bread."

Angel: The devil was trying to trick him. If Jesus couldn't do it, it'd prove he'd been a liar about who he was. But if he did do it, then he'd be depending on his powers, rather than physically relying on God. It was a trap! And after that much time without food, I thought he just might go for it.

Narrator: But Jesus said, "No! The Bible says people must rely on God's word, not just on bread for their lives."

Angel: Whew! It was a good answer. Relying on Scripture makes sense.

Narrator: Then the devil took him to a high mountain and showed Jesus all the kingdoms of the world in a moment's time.

Angel: It was like watching a movie. All these pictures from all over the world flashed in front of Jesus' eyes. We saw 'em, too.

Narrator: And the devil offered him all authority, all rule, over all the kingdoms if only Jesus would worship him.

Angel: Jesus didn't argue with him. I mean, in a way, the devil really is the ruler of this world, even though God Almighty has the final word. . . And to someone just starting out in ministry it must have been tempting—especially when you think about what most preachers make.

Narrator: But Jesus said, "The Bible says we should worship God alone and serve him only. I'm not gonna worship you."

Angel: Two for two. Jesus was really relying on God's Word rather than his own strength. Well, he didn't have much of that left—strength, that is. After all that time without any hamburgers, hotdogs, macaroni and cheese, pizza or ice cream.

Narrator: Then the devil took Jesus to the highest place in the temple. "Go on. If you really are the Son of God, jump off. Doesn't the Bible say God will send his angels to take care of you?! Prove it!"

Angel: I got ready. I figured if Jesus really did jump, I was gonna show the devil once and for all that God's word is true. *(Hold out your arms like you're going to catch someone who's falling)* Go on, Jesus. Prove it to him! I'll catch you! I promise!

Narrator: Jesus just shook his head. "Don't put the Lord your God to the test," he said.

Angel: *(Stand normal again)* Huh. I should've thought of that. Instead of feeling like he had to prove himself, Jesus just stuck with God's Word through everything. Cool.

Narrator: And then, just like that, the devil was gone.

Angel: We knew he'd be back. He always comes back.

Narrator: And angels came to take care of Jesus.

Angel: The devil is sly. He'll come after you when you least expect it.

Narrator: When you're tired or weak—

Angel: And the only way to resist is to lean on God and His Word,

Narrator: Just like Jesus did.

(Freeze. Fade out the stage lights. Exit.)

A Graveyard Story

Based On: Mark 5:1-20

Big Idea: Jesus is more powerful than demons. When Jesus sets us free, we're motivated to follow him too, just like the ex-demoniac was.

Background: Mark records the gripping account of how Jesus cast the demons out of a man who lived among the dead bodies of the tombs. When he was set free from the demons, the man wanted to stay with Jesus, but Jesus told him to go home and tell his family about all that God had done for him. The man became the first Christian missionary to the Decapolis, ten cities in the region of the Gerasenes.

Type: Tandem monologues

Tellers: Peter—A friend of Jesus who witnessed Christ cast out demons (male); Demoniac—A man possessed with many demons that Jesus cast out (male).

Tools: None; or, you may wish to have two musician's stools on stage and have the storytellers seated on the stools for a portion of the story or for the whole performance.

Topics: Conversion, demons, following God, freedom, God's power, Jesus, new life, witnessing

Tips: This story is a little bit more serious and slightly scary. It would make a great campfire story at summer camp or at a lock-in for preteens. Because of its graphic content, use discernment in using this story with younger students. The two storytellers will stay in character as Peter and the Demoniac throughout the entire story. Each person remains frozen while the other storyteller delivers his lines. You may wish to have the storytellers sit on the stools, lean on them, or stand up and walk around at various parts in the story. The storytellers don't make eye contact with each other, but instead, each tells his own story to the audience. Both storytellers start onstage, or enter together. Bring up the stage lights, and then begin when the students are quiet.

Script:

Peter: I was scared, I admit it. We all were. As our boat washed ashore, the mist was still rising off the water. Up ahead, tombs dotted the nearby hills. And that's when we heard the howling.

Demoniac: The days all kinda run together in my mind. Days and months and years. . . . Oh, they tried everything to help me, but nothing worked.

Peter: We climbed out of the boat and stepped onto the wet sand. I gulped as I listened to the strange sounds coming through the fog. I'd heard stories about the madman who lived up there in the hills—we'd all heard the stories.

Demoniac: They tried chaining me up, but I broke through the chains like they were paper. Eventually people just stopped coming—everyone stopped coming. They left me there alone; out there by the tombs and the graves and all the dead bodies.

Peter: Then the Lord called to me, "Hey, Pete, why don't you tie up the boat; we're going ashore." And I was like, "Um, you want us to get out here? By the *(gulp)*. . . tombs?. . ."

Demoniac: I was outta my mind. I know that now. I couldn't control myself. Sometimes I'd slam my head against the tombstones, or I'd just sit there slicing up my body with sharp rocks from the ground. Part of me knew what I was doing. Part of me tried to stop, but I couldn't, no matter how hard I tried. I wasn't in control of myself. Something else was.

Peter: They said it was demons that made him act the way he did. They said that no one was strong enough to stop him. Nothing was strong enough to stop him. Night and day he would roam the hills, moaning and screaming. Attacking himself. Attacking anyone who got in his way.

Demoniac: When the Master stepped ashore, I ran toward him. I'd been sitting in one of the open tombs, next to a rotting corpse, playing with the bones. But I could sense that he was ashore. It was almost like I knew who he was and why he'd come. And as I ran toward him, I knew that the demons inside me wanted me to kill him.

Peter: I was next to the boat when he appeared out of the fog, howling like a madman, running straight toward the Lord. I thought for sure Jesus was a goner. But then. . .

Demoniac: Despite all the hatred boiling inside of me, I crumpled to the ground in front of him.

Peter: I couldn't believe what happened next.

Demoniac: I yelled at the top of my voice, "What do you want with me, Jesus, son of the Most High God? Have you come to torture me?"

Peter: "Come out of this man, you evil spirit!" That's what Jesus said. "Come out of this man!" He wasn't scared—not in the least! And then Jesus asked him his name.

Demoniac: *(Speaking in an evil voice)* "Legion. *(Louder this time)* Legion!"

Peter: I knew it wasn't him talking, but the demons inside him.

Demoniac: *(Speaking in an evil voice)* "We are known as Legion, for we are many."

Peter: Then the demons begged the Lord over and over not to send them out of the region. They were scared of him—you could tell. Scared of what he could do to them.

Demoniac: Nearby, there was this huge herd of pigs. Then the spirits inside of me cried, *(Speaking in an evil voice)* "Send us among the pigs! Let us go into them!"

Peter: Suddenly, the herd of pigs—there was, like, 2000 of 'em—rushed down the steep cliffs and splashed into the lake. Every one of 'em drowned. Every last one. It was horrifying to think of that many demons living inside this one man. . .

Demoniac: The moment he said the word and the demons left, I could feel the change. I was free! Free for the first time in years! It was like I was alive again. I had my life back!

Peter: The villagers gathered around, shocked and amazed. They couldn't believe their eyes and neither could we. The man who'd been raving mad and demon-possessed a few moments ago was sitting at Jesus' feet dressed, and thinking clearly.

Demoniac: They were scared when they saw me. Scared of the power of this humble man in front of me. They begged him to leave. But I wasn't scared of him. For the first time in years, I wasn't scared at all. And I didn't want him to leave me. I wanted to stay with him, close by his side forever.

Peter: As we were getting back on the boat, the man who'd been demon-possessed pleaded to come along. But the Lord said, "No. Go home. Tell your family how much the Lord has done for you. And how he has had mercy on you."

Demoniac: So that's what I did. And that's what I'm still doing. Telling everyone I meet how much he did for me. And all of the people who hear it are amazed at the power of this man of miracles—this man called Jesus.

(Freeze. Fade out the stage lights. Exit.)

Based On: Luke 5:1-11

Big Idea: When we discover the true identity of Jesus, our lives are changed forever.

Background: Even though the first disciples (Peter, Andrew, James, and John) had started to follow Jesus, they hadn't truly recognized who he really was. One day, after a miraculous catch of fish, they left their nets behind and followed Jesus for good. When we recognize the true identity of Christ, our lives are changed forever as well.

Type: Storymime (without audience participation)

Tellers: This is another Bonnie and George story. In this story, George does the actions as Bonnie narrates the story. They make a few opening and closing remarks to the audience.

Tools: None

Topics: Calling, confession, following God, God's power, Jesus, ministry, purpose, sin

Tips: The silent storyteller should be enthusiastic about doing the actions, but keep going too far doing the wrong ones. When the speaking storyteller corrects him, he should nod or acknowledge that he understands. This acknowledgement is recorded in the script with the phrase "Oh." Because of the nature of this storymime, it might work best to just have the silent storyteller do the actions rather than having the students join along. The storytellers could be either men or women. Both storytellers start onstage, or enter together. Bring up the stage lights, and then begin when the students are quiet.

Script:

Bonnie:	Okay, for today's story, one of us will have to do the actions while the other one tells the story.
George:	I'll do the actions!
Bonnie:	Are you sure?
George:	Absolutely.
Bonnie:	You're not gonna mix them up or anything?
George:	Who me? Not a chance.
Bonnie:	You're sure?
George:	Oh, yeah. No problemo. Where do I stand?
Bonnie:	Um. . . You can stand right over there.
George:	*(Walk to another spot on stage.)* Here?
Bonnie:	Yeah.
George:	Okay.
Bonnie:	You ready?
George:	Yup!
Bonnie:	Okay. . . .

What to say:	What to do:
One day, Peter and John were out fishing. . .	*Cast and reel a fishing rod.*
With their nets.	**(Oh.)** *Toss nets toward audience.*
All night long.	*Yawn and continue to toss nets.*
But they didn't catch anything.	*Fall asleep and snore.*
Um. . . they didn't fall asleep.	*Wake up and stretch your arms.*
In the morning, they were sitting on shore, cleaning and brushing their—	*Brush your teeth.*
Nets.	**(Oh.)** *Brush off the nets.*
Now, nearby Jesus was preaching to the crowds—	*Point, posture, and act like a preacher.*
Not directing a choir, preaching to the crowds and telling them stories.	**(Oh.)** *Act like a Shakespearean actor.*
The crowds were so big Jesus didn't have a place to stand.	*Repeat dramatic gestures, this time very tiny.*
So, Peter let him stand on his boat.	*Rock back and forth and fall over.*
Um. . . they didn't fall in the water.	**(Oh.)** *Stand back up. Rock back and forth.*
They pushed off from shore.	*Push off with an oar.*
After Jesus excused the crowd.	*Wave goodbye.*
He told Peter to drop the net.	*Mime dropping a net on your feet. Hop around holding your foot.*
Not on his foot, off the side of the boat. . .	*Drop the net off the side of the boat.*
Um, the other side of the boat.	**(Oh.)** *Mime dropping the net off the other side of the boat.*
And the net began to fill with fish.	*Make fish lips and pretend to swim.*
Peter dropped to his knees and worshipped Jesus.	*Drop to your knees and clasp hands in prayer.*
As the nets filled with fish—	*Make fish lips and pretend to swim.*
The boat began to tip.	*Lean way over to one side.*
Not that much.	**(Oh.)** *Straighten up. As she looks away, tip over again.*
***(Noticing him)* I said, not that much. . .**	**(Oh.)** *Straighten up again. As she looks away, tip over again.*
Peter rowed back to shore.	*Row.*
Um. . . shore is that way.	**(Oh.)** *Turn around and row again.*

Now, when they arrived, they got off the boat.	*Climb out of the boat.*
They left their nets full of fish. . .	*Make fish lips and pretend to swim.*
And, stepping ashore, they followed Jesus. And it changed their lives forever. . .	*Walk in place.*
The end.	*Bow.*

Bonnie: Well, that wasn't too bad, George.

George: Wait a minute, Bonnie. Are you telling me they left their nets full of fish to follow Jesus!?

Bonnie: Uh-huh.

George: But, they were fishermen! This was the catch of a lifetime! How could they do that?!

Bonnie: They had bigger fish to fry.

George: What are you talking about?

Bonnie: Jesus was calling them to fish for people. To bring people into his kingdom. He was calling them to a whole new way of life.

George: And they left their nets behind. . . .

Bonnie: Yup.

George: So, when we follow Jesus, are we supposed to leave our old lives behind, too?

Bonnie: Well. . . yes, and no. I mean, Paul kept making tents after he became a believer. Luke remained a doctor. The point of this story is that they finally decided to follow Jesus wholeheartedly, with no turning back. And that's what God wants us to do.

George: So we need to leave behind anything that might distract us from following Jesus with all of our hearts.

Bonnie: You got it.

George: Good. Now, wanna go fishing?

Bonnie: Why not? As long as you promise not to mess things up.

George: Who me? Not a chance. . .

(Fade out the stage lights as the storytellers exit.)

Rappelling Through the Roof

17

Based On: Mark 2:1-12

Big Idea: Jesus has the power not only to heal our bodies, but to forgive sins as well.

Background: Early in Jesus' ministry he was turning heads because of his amazing power and unusual claims. In this story, he shows that he not only has power over diseases, but also the worst disease of all—sin. We also see that nothing should get in the way of us bringing our friends to Jesus.

Type: Tandem storytelling

Tellers: Bonnie—A serious storyteller trying to tell the story correctly (female or male); George—Her friend, who keeps getting everything mixed up (male or female).

Tools: None

Topics: Faith, forgiveness, friendship, God's power, Jesus, priorities

Tips: Both storytellers start onstage, or enter together. Bring up the stage lights, and then begin when the students are quiet.

Script

Bonnie: Today's story is one of the coolest and funniest and weirdest stories about Jesus.

George: That's right, Bonnie. I love this story!

Bonnie: Do you even know what story this is?

George: Of course I do! Um. . . it's the story of. . . um. . . .

Bonnie: You don't have a clue, do you?

George: Not a one.

Bonnie: I didn't think so. Now, it happened in Capernaum. Jesus had just arrived and word spread quickly.

George: Pretty soon, the news crews were out and everything. *(Start hitting your chest with your hands)*

Bonnie: What are you doing?

George: Helicopter. Channel 12 News.

Bonnie: There was no helicopter!

George: Oh. *(Stop it)*

Bonnie: Now, the crowd was so packed in that not even one more person could fit through the door.

George: So they all got into the helicopter.

Bonnie: Now, there were these four guys carrying their friend on a mat.

George: Their friend's name was Matt.

Bonnie: No, his name wasn't Matt. He was lying on a mat.

George: He was lying on a guy named Matt! Poor guy.

Bonnie: No, they were carrying one man on a mat. Not a person, a mat. Like a cot or a sleeping bag. And they tried to get in past the crowd of people.

George: And the guy on the mat couldn't get up because there were too many people.

Bonnie: Actually, he couldn't get up because he was paralyzed.

George: He was?

Bonnie:	Yeah, and his friends were trying to bring him to Jesus. And they weren't going to let a little thing like a packed house get in the way.
George:	So what'd they do?
Bonnie:	They climbed up on the roof—
George:	Why didn't they just use the helicopter!
Bonnie:	There was no helicopter! And when they got up there they began to dig through the roof.
George:	What!? Wait a minute. You're telling me they just started digging through the roof?
Bonnie:	Yup.
George:	What were they gonna do? Rappel down? Bungee jump? Geronimo!
Bonnie:	No, they tied ropes to the guy's mat.
George:	That had to hurt.
Bonnie:	Matt wasn't a person!
George:	Who was he?
Bonnie:	*(Sigh and then continue)* Then they started lowering him down through the hole in the roof.
George:	And all this was going on right in the middle of Jesus' sermon?!
Bonnie:	Yup.
George:	I've been in some sermons that coulda' used something like that.
Bonnie:	What, as an object lesson?
George:	No, to keep me awake.
Bonnie:	Oh.
George:	That guy must have been scared out of his wits thinking, "If these guys aren't careful I might tip off this mat and land on the ground and break both my legs and be paralyzed for life!"
Bonnie:	He was already paralyzed for life.
George:	Oh, yeah. That's right.
Bonnie:	So they lowered him down, right in front of Jesus. *(Trying to be funny)* I guess you could say they brought down the house! *(Laugh at your own joke)*
George:	*(Don't laugh)*
Bonnie:	Brought down the house. Get it?
George:	I get it. It just wasn't that funny.
Bonnie:	Oh. . . And when Jesus saw what kind of faith these guys had, he was impressed and he said, "Friend, your sins are forgiven."
George:	But I thought they'd come to get him healed. Isn't that right?
Bonnie:	Yeah, but Jesus was taking care of the most important thing first. It's much more important that we have faith and find forgiveness than whether or not we can walk around.
George:	It is?
Bonnie:	Sure. It's the most important thing of all.
George:	Oh, yeah. I guess you're right. I never thought of that before.
Bonnie:	Now, when all the Pharisees heard him say that—
George:	What's a swimming ferret have to do with anything?
Bonnie:	What?
George:	You said, "All the ferrets in the sea."
Bonnie:	No, I said Pharisees. A Pharisee was a religious ruler in Jesus' day.
George:	They weren't furry little animals?
Bonnie:	No. But they were very concerned about following all the Jewish rules. And sometimes they forgot that our faith is what makes us right with God, not how well we meet a bunch of religious requirements.

George:	Oh. I thought you said "ferrets."
Bonnie:	I know.
George:	A ferret is a furry little woodland creature.
Bonnie:	Yes, I know that.
George:	They don't have anything to do with healing paralyzed guys on mats.
Bonnie:	No, they don't.
George:	And they don't live in the oceans either.
Bonnie:	Were you even listening to me?
George:	Um. . . Yeah. Pharisees. Very religious. Worried about rules. Gotcha.
Bonnie:	Okay, so when they heard what Jesus said about forgiveness, they thought, "Only God can forgive someone else's sin!"
George:	Huh. They were right about that.
Bonnie:	Yes, they were. And since Jesus claimed to do it, they assumed he was claiming to be—
George:	God himself!
Bonnie:	Right. And he said, "It's easier to heal bones than souls. But to show you that I can do the hard thing, I'll do the easy one, too. Then, you'll know that I really can forgive sins."
George:	And then he turned to the guy and said, "Stand up. Pick up that mat of yours and go home."
Bonnie:	Yup, and then the man leapt to his feet, picked up his mat and began to push his way through the crowd.
George:	Everyone there was amazed.
Bonnie:	Right.
George:	Because of how easily he was carrying that guy named Matt and his pet ferret.
Bonnie:	*(Shake your head)* And they began to praise and thank God. No one had seen anything like that before.
George:	I'll say. Especially the insurance adjusters.
Bonnie:	Huh?
George:	The insurance guys. You know. For the roof. I mean, who was gonna pay to fix that?
Bonnie:	The Bible doesn't say. And it really doesn't matter.
George:	What! What do you mean it doesn't matter? What if it snowed or something? It would totally ruin the linoleum!
Bonnie:	They didn't have linoleum.
George:	Carpeting?
Bonnie:	Look, forgiveness is what matters most. Remember?
George:	Oh, yeah.
Bonnie:	So maybe it was the friends who paid for it. Maybe the guy. Maybe Jesus. Maybe the person who owned the house.
George:	*(Realizing the truth)* Because houses don't matter much at all compared to sins being forgiven or paralyzed people being healed.
Bonnie:	Right.
George:	Huh. So what ever happened to Matt?
Bonnie:	Who?
George:	The guy who owns the swimming ferrets. Did he ever go rappelling again?
Bonnie:	*(Sighing)* Why do I put up with this?

(Exit. Fade out the stage lights.)

The Last Supper

Based On: Luke 22:7-23 and John 13:21-30

Big Idea: Jesus instituted the Lord's Supper as a special way for us to remember him and proclaim his death until he comes.

Background: On the night Jesus was betrayed, he met with his closest friends to celebrate the Jewish Passover meal. During the meal, Jesus identified his betrayer and instituted a new covenant or agreement between God and people. This special meal is a way of acknowledging our faith, our unity, and the forgiveness that comes through Christ alone.

Type: Narralogue

Tellers: Narrator—a storyteller who tells the story of the last supper (male or female); John/Judas—a storyteller who plays the part of both the apostles John and Judas, giving their own perspectives on the events of the Last Supper (male).

Tools: None; or you may wish to have bread and juice to hold up at various places in the story when the Lord's Supper is explained. You may wish to have a small costume piece such as a hat, dark sunglasses, or a scarf for the storyteller who plays the part of John and Judas to wear during his respective parts.

Topics: Faith, forgiveness, friendship, Jesus, Judas, Lord's Supper, Passover, sin, worship

Tips: This story is one of the more serious ones in this collection. Some Bible scholars believe that Judas was present during the Lord's Supper, others believe he left the meal before Jesus instituted the ceremony. You may wish to reorder the events in this story to emphasize one of the two opinions. This story could be told by three storytellers, using separate people for John and Judas. If you choose to use three storytellers, John and Judas turn their backs to the audience when they're parts are done. You may wish to have the storytellers sit on stools or hold up the bread and juice (or wine) during the story. Both storytellers start onstage, or enter together. Bring up the stage lights, and then begin when the students are quiet.

Script

Narrator: Before Jesus was captured and led away to be put to death, he met with his friends to celebrate the Jewish Passover meal.

John: We were all gathered together for supper. Now, we didn't eat at tables like you do today. Instead, we lounged on the floor, leaning on one elbow *(if you are on a stage, say, "like this" and demonstrate)*.

Narrator: While they were eating, Jesus became very sad and said, "My friends, one of you is going to betray me."

John: We whispered among ourselves, "Who is it? Who is he talking about?" We had no idea who it could be.

Narrator: Jesus was lounging next to two of his closest friends, John and Judas. Sitting next to John was Peter.

John: So finally, Pete whispered to me, "Hey, John, ask him who it is." So I leaned close to Jesus, so that my head was almost laying on his chest, and I said, "Who is it, Jesus? Who is going to betray you?" *(Turn your back to the audience and freeze. When you say your next lines, you are going to be delivering them as Judas rather than as John.)*

Narrator: Jesus explained that he would give some food to the man who would betray him. Then he handed his food to Judas.

Judas: He'd hinted earlier that it might be me. I don't think anyone really made the connection, though. I don't know how he could have known about the plan.

Narrator: Judas had made arrangements with the Jewish leaders to hand Jesus over to them for 30 pieces of silver.

Judas: I watched as Jesus gave me that piece of food. And I said, "You don't mean me, do you, Jesus?" He just looked at me. . .

Narrator: Judas was in charge of the money for the group. He was one of Jesus' most trusted apostles, so no one suspected he might be the one.

Judas: Then he lowered his voice and said, "It is you, Judas. You're the one." As soon as he said it, I got up. And as I did he said, "What you've planned to do, do quickly." Did he really know? Had he found out?! I wasn't sure, but I headed for the door. *(Turn your back to the audience and freeze. When you say your next lines, you are going to be delivering them as John again rather than as Judas.)*

Narrator: During the meal, Jesus took the bread and said a little prayer and then handed it to his disciples.

John: We thought maybe he was talking about having Judas buy something for us for the Passover. We didn't really understand. It didn't seem possible that our friend Judas could really betray Jesus.

Narrator: The bread they used back then wasn't soft and fluffy, but crispy, like a cracker. So, Jesus broke it in half.

John: As Jesus passed around the bread, he said, "Go on, eat some. This bread is my body and it's broken to make you whole. From now on, when you break it and eat it, think of me."

Narrator: Long ago, God's people had been slaves in Egypt. God made a special promise to his people. Each family killed a lamb and put the blood on the doorframe of their home. Then, when God's angel saw the blood, he would pass over the house. No harm would come to them.

John: Jesus said it was his body that was broken. What about the Passover lamb? What was Jesus trying to say?

Narrator: Then, after supper, he took the cup of wine and thanked his father for it.

John: He passed it around and said, "Go on, have a drink. This wine is the blood of the new agreement. It's poured out for many people—to forgive their sins. Whenever you drink it, think of me."

Narrator: His friends listened to him and took some bread and wine. And as they did, they were all thinking carefully about the words he had said.

John: Then, I remembered what John the Baptist used to say, about Jesus being the Lamb of God—the one who takes away the sin of the world. And I finally began to understand. He is the Lamb.

Narrator: Jesus told them that his body and blood were forming a new agreement between people and God.

John: He's the real Lamb of God. And his blood does take away the sin of the world. It all started to make sense!

Narrator: Then, Jesus told his friends he wouldn't be drinking grape juice or wine with them again until they all had a reunion in heaven.

John: Then, we sang a hymn and headed out to the garden of Gethsemane.

(Freeze. Exit together. Fade out the stage lights.)

At the Scene of the Grave

Based On: Mark 16 and John 20:1-18

Big Idea: Three days after dying, Jesus rose from the dead, just as he'd predicted he would. He took our penalty on himself and rose so that we could know our sins are forgiven when we trust in him.

Background: Each of the gospel writers records what happened at the scene of the tomb in his own words. Together they give us a complete picture of the people whom Jesus appeared to after his resurrection. The best news of all is that Jesus rose from the dead so that we could have eternal life with God.

Type: Interview

Tellers: Mary of Magdala—One of Jesus' followers and the first person to see Jesus alive after he rose from the dead (female); Les Braincell—A corny detective investigating the report of a missing body in a graveyard near Jerusalem (male).

Tools: A trench coat, notepad, and magnifying glass for Les

Topics: Easter, God's love, grace, Jesus, new life, prophecy fulfillment

Tips: Les Braincell's character is meant to be corny, so ham it up, be goofy, exaggerated, and silly. Since he appears in several sketches, you may wish to use a costume that he could wear whenever he tells one of these stories. Les starts the scene onstage. Bring up the stage lights, and then begin when the students are quiet.

Script

Les: I'm Les, Les Braincell here, the world's greatest detective dude. I'm on the scene in this graveyard . . . *(looking around)* I don't like graveyards. . . But I'm not afraid.

Mary: *(Enter, Mary)* Boo.

Les: Ah! *(Fall over and act crazy as if really scared)* What are you doing, sneaking up on me like that! Who do you think you are?

Mary: Mary.

Les: Aha! Just as I suspected! Where were you on August 22 at 5:00 p.m.?

Mary: Um. . . I don't know. . .

Les: Aha! So you might have been stealing the body!

Mary: Um, what body?

Les: Acting innocent, huh? Well, I can play that game, too. I'm telling you, it wasn't me. I didn't do it!

Mary: Do what?

Les: Steal the candy from my mother's vase on the table when I was 8 years old. Okay, I did it! You broke me! I can't take the pressure. I did it! I'm guilty! Take me away!

Mary: Um, what are you talking about?

Les: Oh. You aren't from the FBI. That's good. *(Flipping open a notebook)* So, what did you say your name is?

Mary: Um. . . Mary of Magdala.

Les: So, you refuse to tell me your last name!

Mary:	I don't have one.
Les:	A likely story. What do I look like, an idiot?! A nincompoop?! A numbskull?! Wait, don't answer that.
Mary:	Okay.
Les:	So, Mary who?
Mary:	Huh?
Les:	You.
Mary:	Who?
Les:	You who?
Mary:	You who to you, too!
Les:	Huh?
Mary:	Me?
Les:	Who are you?
Mary:	Who are you?
Les:	I'm Les, Les Braincell—wait a minute. Very sneaky. I'm the one who's supposed to be asking the questions around here! What are you doing sneaking through a graveyard in the middle of the night?
Mary:	It's not the middle of the night. It's daybreak.
Les:	Trying to overwhelm me with details, huh? Well, it won't work! I'm as sharp as. . . as. . .
Mary:	A marble?
Les:	Right! Now, where were we?
Mary:	In the graveyard!
Les:	I don't like graveyards.
Mary:	Boo.
Les:	Ah!
Mary:	Hee, hee, hee. . .
Les:	Did you see a ghost?
Mary:	No.
Les:	So you admit it then!
Mary:	I admit what?
Les:	You admit that you didn't see a ghost! Now, we're getting somewhere!
Mary:	What are you talking about?
Les:	I have no idea.
Mary:	I didn't see any ghosts, but I did see a man.
Les:	Was his name Les Braincell?
Mary:	No.
Les:	You mean I've changed my name?
Mary:	I saw Jesus.
Les:	Now, I know you're lying to me! Jesus was killed over 2000 years ago! *(Begin to arrest her)* C'mon, I'm taking you in!
Mary:	Um. . . He was only killed a few days ago.
Les:	He was?
Mary:	Yes.
Les:	What year is it?
Mary:	33 A.D.
Les:	Hmm. . . . I must have taken a wrong turn in Kalamazoo. . . . What day is it?

Mary:	It's Sunday morning.
Les:	Aha!
Mary:	Aha, what? Why did you say "aha!"?
Les:	I have no idea. . .. Oh, wait! Aha! I know! So, you say you saw Jesus?
Mary:	Yes, in the flesh. So to speak.
Les:	And he was alive?!
Mary:	Yes.
Les:	Was he carrying a dead body by any chance? Someone reported a missing body this morning.
Mary:	Um. . . That was Jesus' body that was missing.
Les:	So, now we have a missing person and a missing body. It's a good thing I'm here.
Mary:	Why is that?
Les:	Because I'm Les, Les Braincell, the world's greatest detective dude.
Mary:	Oh. But Jesus isn't missing.
Les:	He's not?
Mary:	No. And no one stole his body.
Les:	They didn't?
Mary:	No. He came back from the dead.
Les:	Aha! CPR!
Mary:	Um, no. God brought him back to life.
Les:	God performed CPR on a missing person?
Mary:	No.
Les:	So. . . It's all God's fault.
Mary:	Um, it's not God's fault. Nothing went wrong. It was his plan all along.
Les:	His plan, huh. So it was premeditated.
Mary:	Look, I have to go.
Les:	Wait. So, you say Jesus is alive?
Mary:	Yes!
Les:	Well, you have to admit it's a little farfetched, to believe that somebody's gonna be killed, dead as a doorknob, and then three days later come back to life.
Mary:	That's right! It is farfetched. And that's why I'm so excited.
Les:	Because it's the biggest news story of all time!
Mary:	You can say that again.
Les:	Because it's the biggest news story—
Mary:	Um, it's a figure of speech.
Les:	Oh.
Mary:	Look, I'm on my way to tell John and Peter and the rest of Jesus' friends that he isn't dead, but alive. Just as he said he would be. Wanna come?
Les:	Absolutely. Then I can solve this case once and for all! . . . Um, are you positive there aren't any ghosts out here?
Mary:	Boo.
Les:	Ah! Stop doing that!
Mary:	Hee, hee, hee. . . .

(Fade out the stage lights as the storytellers exit.)

24 Tandem Bible Story Scripts for Children's Ministry

Tongues of Fire

20

Based On:	Acts 2
Big Idea:	God sent the Holy Spirit to the first disciples at Pentecost. He still sends His Spirit to all believers today.
Background:	After Jesus rose into the sky following his resurrection from the dead, the believers gathered to await the sending of the Holy Spirit. Finally, seven weeks after Jesus' resurrection, the Spirit came upon the believers in power and about 3000 people were converted in one day. The early church continued to grow quickly through the power and guidance of the Holy Spirit.
Type:	Tandem storytelling
Tellers:	Dana—A slightly more serious storyteller trying to tell the story correctly (female or male); Matt—Her friend, who occasionally gets things mixed up (male or female).
Tools:	None
Topics:	Baptism, conversion, Holy Spirit, Pentecost, Peter, prophecy fulfillment, repentance, witnessing
Tips:	Note that the storytellers sometimes say their lines together. Both storytellers start onstage, or enter together. Bring up the stage lights, and then begin when the students are quiet.

Script:

Dana:	After Jesus went to heaven,
Matt:	The disciples gathered together,
Together:	To pray.
Dana:	And to wait for the Holy Spirit.
Matt:	So they waited—
Dana:	And waited—
Matt:	And waited—
Dana:	And waited—
Matt:	Until seven weeks had passed,
Dana:	From the time Jesus rose from the dead.
Matt:	Then all the believers were gathered together in Jerusalem.
Dana:	And there were many other people in town as well.
Matt:	Parthians, Medes, and Elamites.
Dana:	People from Mesopotamia, Judea, and Cappadocia.
Matt:	Folks from Pontus, Asia, and Phrygia.
Dana:	Pamphylia, Egypt, and Libya.
Matt:	Romans and Cretans and Arabs.
Dana:	Whew!
Matt:	No kidding.
Dana:	And that day, early in the morning—

Matt:	While they were praying—
Dana:	There was the sound of a mighty wind!
Matt:	*(Make wind sounds and blow in Dana's face)* Whoosh!
Dana:	That was mighty, alright.
Matt:	Thank you.
Dana:	Mighty strong.
Matt:	Yes, it was.
Dana:	Smelling.
Matt:	Huh?
Dana:	Strong smelling. Mighty strong smelling. Get yourself a breath mint or something. Whew, mama!
Matt:	Oh.
Dana:	And then, little tongues of fire appeared on the believers' heads.
Matt:	*(Stick out tongue repeatedly like a lizard)*
Dana:	Not that kind of tongue.
Matt:	Oh. Okay. *(Wiggle your fingers on your head)*
Dana:	Right. They were little flames of fire.
Matt:	And the believers began to speak in all types of languages.
Dana:	The languages of. . .
Matt:	*(Say the names faster this time)* Parthians, Medes, and Elamites.
Dana:	People from Mesopotamia, Judea, and Cappadocia.
Matt:	Folks from Pontus, Asia, and Phrygia.
Dana:	Pamphylia, Egypt, and Libya.
Matt:	Romans and Cretans and Arabs.
Dana:	Whew!
Matt:	No kidding.
Dana:	And each person heard the believers speaking to them,
Matt:	In his—
Dana:	Or her—
Matt:	Own language.
Dana:	It was amazing!
Matt:	And some of the people thought that maybe the disciples had been out drinking the night before.
Dana:	But Peter said,
Matt:	"No! We haven't been to the bars! God's Spirit is speaking through us. Just like the prophet Joel predicted. When he said. . .."
Dana:	"God will pour out his Spirit on all people, and anyone who calls on the name of the Lord will be saved."
Matt:	*(Continue preaching as Peter)* "Jesus of Nazareth came from God himself. And you and the Gentiles had him murdered. But God raised him back to life. For death couldn't hold him. It's like King David wrote. . . ."
Dana:	"You will not let him rot away in the grave."
Matt:	"See? David was talking about Jesus. And now God has poured out his Holy Spirit on us."
Dana:	*(Narrating)* Then Peter told them that Jesus was both the Lord and the promised Savior.
Matt:	And the people who heard this were deeply sorry and asked,
Dana:	"What shall we do, brothers?"

Matt:	*(Respond as Peter)* "Turn to God. Turn away from sin, and be baptized in the name of Jesus Christ for the forgiveness of your sins. Then you'll receive the Holy Spirit, both you and your children and everyone everywhere who believes in the Lord!"
Dana:	Then Peter went on to preach for a long time. *(Turn to Matt)* But, um, you don't have to do that for us here today.
Matt:	Okay.
Dana:	And Peter begged them to listen to him and to trust in the Lord. And that day, many people believed and were baptized.
Matt:	About 3000 people in all.
Dana:	Then they came together with the other believers—
Matt:	For prayer,
Dana:	And teaching,
Matt:	And the Lord's Supper,
Together:	And for fellowship.
Dana:	From then on, the believers met together and shared everything they had with those in need.
Matt:	Every day they worshiped together,
Dana:	Prayed to God,
Matt:	And enjoyed his goodness.
Dana:	And every day, their number grew bigger—
Matt:	And bigger—
Dana:	And bigger.
Matt:	With people from all over—
Dana:	Oh, no. Not again.
Matt:	Yup!
Dana:	No, please, no.
Matt:	One more time!
Dana:	Okay. . .
Matt:	Parthians, Medes, and Elamites.
Dana:	People from Mesopotamia, Judea, and Cappadocia.
Matt:	Folks from Pontus, Asia, and Phrygia.
Dana:	Pamphylia, Egypt, and Libya.
Matt:	Romans and Cretans and Arabs.
Dana:	Whew!
Matt:	No kidding.
Together:	The end.

(Bow. Fade out the stage lights. Exit.)

When Tabitha Got Sew Sick. . . She Dyed

Based On: Acts 9:36-43

Big Idea: Through God's power, Peter raised Tabitha, a generous and faithful woman, back to life.

Background: Tabitha, a kindhearted woman who was generous to the poor, lived in Joppa. After she died, the disciples showed amazing faith by calling Peter to her home. After praying for her, he raised Tabitha from the dead and many people from that area believed in the Lord.

Type: Tandem storytelling with audience participation

Tellers: Bonnie—A serious storyteller trying to tell the story correctly (female or male); George—Her friend, who keeps getting everything mixed up (male or female).

Tools: None; or you may wish to have a wig for the person who plays the part of Tabitha

Topics: Death, faith, friendship, generosity, God's power, grief and loss, new life, Peter, prayer

Tips: Throughout this story, George is rhyming nearly everything he says, ala Dr. Seuss. This story also includes a lot of audience involvement and would be best used with a larger group so that there are plenty of people in the audience to watch the show. In the script, wherever ellipses (". . .") occur in the narration sections, pause and allow the actors on stage enough time to do the actions. The storytellers could be either men or women. Both storytellers start onstage, or enter together. Bring up the stage lights, and then begin when the students are quiet.

Script

Bonnie: Okay, today's story is about a lady named Tabitha, and we're going to use some audience members in the show. *(Search the audience for a guy to play the role of Peter. Then point to him and continue)* Okay, you be Peter.

George: He be Pete.

Bonnie: Right.

George: Pete he be.

Bonnie: Um. . . right.

George: Would you like to play with me?

Bonnie: What are you doing?

George: I will rhyme.

Bonnie: That's nice.

George: All the time.

Bonnie: Okay.

George: Because I know it's not a crime!

Bonnie: Look, just wait with your rhyming until we start. Stand over there while I get some other people to help us with this story.

George: I will stand.

Bonnie:	Good.
George:	On the land.
Bonnie:	Oh, great.
George:	Would you like to shake my hand?

(Bonnie goes through the audience, choosing one person to be the "doorway," two girls to be "weeping widows," two people to be the "disciples" and a large boy or a man to be Tabitha. For fun, give him a wig to wear. As you do this, say something like. . . **"Okay, you be the doorway and you be the weeping widows. . . you two be the two disciples. . . and you be Tabitha."** *As you begin, position Peter off to the left of the stage and the disciples off to the right of the stage; the rest of the people can begin on center stage.)*

Bonnie:	Once, long ago, there was a lady who lived in Joppa and her name was Tabitha.
George:	*(Pointing to the man playing the part of Tabitha)* He be she.
Bonnie:	Tabitha.
George:	She be he.
Bonnie:	Right.
George:	That be one big girl, you see. Hee, bee, jee, bee, jee, bee, jee.
Bonnie:	And she would make clothes *(Pause, and, if necessary, encourage Tabitha to pretend to sew)* and give them away to the poor.
George:	I be poor.
Bonnie:	You can stop that now.
George:	Poor I be. Would you give some clothes to me?
Bonnie:	Okay, so one day Tabitha got sick *(Pause and give Tabitha time to act sick. Each time you say it, let her act it out)* Really sick. . . Even sicker. . .
George:	She be sick. Sick she be.
Bonnie:	That's enough already.
George:	Please do not throw up on me.
Bonnie:	She got so sick, she died. . . She fell to the floor and her friends—that's you, weeping widows—washed her body. . . *(Pause and give the widows time to act this out. If appropriate, say, "Just hose her off or something. . .")* And carried her to an upstairs room. . . . *(Pause again. Let them struggle with carrying him. The bigger the Tabitha, the funnier the scene!)* They opened the door. . . and set her inside. . .
George:	*(As they carry her away)* She be dead. Dead she be. Do not drop that girl on me!
Bonnie:	When they found out that Peter was in a nearby city, they sent two disciples to go and get him. . . They told Peter, "Come at once!". . . So, Peter went with them back to Joppa. . . .
George:	Wait a minute. . . Why did they do that if she was already dead?
Bonnie:	Well, they knew that with God's power, anything is possible.
George:	You mean, they wanted her raised back from the dead?
Bonnie:	Yup.
George:	Whoa. God be strong. Strong he be. He be much more strong than me.
Bonnie:	So then, Peter and the disciples arrived in Joppa and all the ladies stood around crying. . .
George:	They be sad. Sad they be. They be sad because of she.
Bonnie:	When Peter arrived, they took him upstairs to the room where Tabitha was lying. . . They opened the door. . . And walked inside. . . and all the women were sitting around crying. . . and looking at the clothes Tabitha had made while she was alive. . . and then Peter—
George:	He be Pete. Pete he be. He not be as dead as *(Point to Tabitha)* she.

Bonnie: Peter sent the women and the men out of the room. . . Don't forget to close the door. . . And then, he got down on his knees. . . and prayed. . . Finally, he turned to the dead woman and said, "Tabitha, get up!". . . She opened her eyes. . . looked up at Peter. . . and sat up. . .

George: She be back! Back she be! She not be so dead you see!

Bonnie: And Peter took her by the hand. . . and helped her to her feet. . . He took her downstairs to the rest of the people. . . Don't forget to close the door. . . and everyone was amazed! *(Pause)* Let's give all our actors and actresses a great big hand for a job well done!

George: They done well! Well they done! And we had a lot of fun!

Bonnie: *(After the actors and actresses have been seated)* Well, George, do you know what the story can teach us today?

George: Well, Bonnie, it shows us that God is more powerful even than death. And that when we pray, he hears us even if it's for something unusual or unbelievable.

Bonnie: You got it. Good job!

George: *(As they exit)* Hey, next time, can I be Pete? I be Pete. Pete I be. Would you eat green eggs with me?

Bonnie: I know what author your momma used to read you when you were a kid.

George: Do you know? Is it so? Was it Edgar Allen Poe?

Bonnie: Um. . . No. . . .

(Fade out the stage lights as the storytellers exit.)

Based On: Acts 10-11:18

Big Idea: God's word is meant for all people everywhere and salvation can come to anyone who believes in Jesus.

Background: At first, the Jews in the early church thought that the message of salvation was meant only for them. Then, through a series of visions and a dramatic encounter with a Roman centurion, Peter realized that God doesn't show favoritism (Acts 10:34-35 and 11:18). Instead, God wants all people every where to trust in him.

Type: Tandem monologues

Tellers: Peter—A Jewish apostle who discovers God's word is intended even for Gentiles (male); Soldier—A devout friend of Cornelius, the centurion, who went to bring Peter back to Cornelius (male, or perhaps female).

Tools: None; or you may wish to have two musician's stools on stage and have the storytellers seated on the stools for a portion of the story or for the whole performance.

Topics: Angels, conversion, faith, following God, forgiveness, generosity, grace, Holy Spirit, Peter, prejudice, witnessing, worship

Tips: This story is a little bit more serious. The two storytellers will stay in character as Peter and the Soldier throughout the entire story. Each person remains frozen while the other storyteller delivers his lines. You may wish to have the storytellers sit on the stools, lean on them, or stand up and walk around at various parts in the story. The storytellers don't make eye contact with each other, but instead, each tells his own story to the audience. Both storytellers begin onstage, seated on musician's stools (if desired) or enter together. Bring up the stage lights, and then begin when the students are quiet.

Script:

Soldier: Cornelius called me into the room, along with two servants and told us his story. And I have to admit, at first I thought it was pretty far-fetched.

Peter: We were close to Joppa that day. I went up on the roof to pray. Yeah, I know it sounds a little weird, but it was quiet up there, and there weren't too many distractions.

Soldier: Well, Cornelius and his family all believed in God and did their best to serve him. They gave to the poor and prayed regularly. But still, when someone starts telling you about a vision where he saw an angel, you kinda wonder if maybe he'd been playing football without his helmet again. I mean, the whole thing was kinda corny, even for Cornelius.

Peter: It was about noon and, man, was I hungry. I could smell the meal cooking down in the house. Oh, it smelled so good. I could just about taste it. Oh, be still, my tummy, be still!

Soldier: So Cornelius says he saw this angel, right? I mean, he's a centurion, so he's been in battles. He's been in charge of soldiers for years. He's seen some really frightening stuff. But this angel freaked him out. He was terrified.

Peter: So anyway, there I was, up on the roof listening to my stomach growl, smelling dinner cooking downstairs. And I started to slip into a trance.

Soldier: The angel told Cornelius that God had seen his good deeds and heard his prayers and wanted him to send some men to Joppa. The angel was like, "Send some men to Joppa! Get Peter here quickly! He's staying with Simon the tanner, whose house is by the sea." Then the angel disappeared.

Peter: I could see heaven opening up and something like a huge blankie coming down. And it had all sorts of animals in it. Alligators, beavers, skunks, possums, porcupines, rattlesnakes, vultures, elephants, llamas, zebras, tadpoles, lizards, eagles, buffalo. You name it, it had it. Then I heard a voice. "Yo, Peter, get up on your feet. Go, kill, and get a bite to eat."

Soldier: Then, Cornelius told us to head to Joppa. So we did. We believed him and started on our way. We weren't sure what to expect.

Peter: I told the voice, "No way! Our laws say we can't eat some of that stuff. It's against the religious rules." But the voice said, "Yo, Peter, this is what I mean, do not call 'dirty' what God has called 'clean.' " This whole vision thing with the Godzilla-sized blankie happened three times, and then I woke up.

Soldier: So we arrived at Simon the Tanner's house and stopped by the gate. There was this tall bearded guy standing on the roof looking confused.

Peter: So there I was, standing on the roof, looking confused. And God's Spirit told me there were three guys down there looking for me. I climbed down and said, "I'm the guy you're looking for. What do you want?"

Soldier: We told Peter all about how Cornelius had sent us and what a good guy he was and how the angel had told us find Peter. And then, Peter invited us into the house.

Peter: The next day, we all started out for Cornelius' house. Six Jewish believers came with us.

Soldier: Cornelius was waiting for us. He'd called all his friends and relatives together. When Peter walked in, Cornelius just dropped down before him.

Peter: I told the guy to stand up and stop trying to worship me. "Get up! I'm just a person like you are!" It was weird for me to talk to him or even go into his house. I mean, he was a Gentile and, well. . . Jews, we just don't do that. But that vision had really opened up my eyes.

Soldier: Then Cornelius repeated the story about the angel and what the angel had told him. "Send some men to Joppa! Get Peter here quickly! He's staying with Simon the tanner, whose house is by the sea." And he said to Peter, "Whatever God wants you to tell us, we're all ears."

Peter: So I told 'em about my vision. And the giant blankie, and all the critters inside, and how that voice had said, "Yo, Peter, this is what I mean, do not call 'dirty' what God has called 'clean.'" " And I explained that God was trying to tell me that he wants all people everywhere to hear the message about Jesus—not just Jews. Nobody should be left out.

Soldier: Peter told us all about Jesus of Nazareth. And we believed. All of us did. And we all got baptized. Then we had a great time talking with Peter and his friends for the next couple of days, learning more and more about Jesus.

Peter: Nope, it doesn't matter where you live,

Soldier: It doesn't matter where you're from.

Peter: Everyone who believes in Jesus receives forgiveness of sins through his name. *(Acts 10:43)*

Soldier: That's what I learned that day.

Peter: That's what I finally learned.

(Exit. Fade out the stage lights.)

Who Can That Be Knocking at My Door?

23

Based On: Acts 12:1-19

Big Idea: God answered the prayers of the believers and set Peter free from prison. God still answers the prayers of believers today.

Background: As the early church grew in size, persecution became more and more intense. King Herod arrested Peter, planning to put him to death as he had done to James, the brother of John. When the believers prayed for Peter, neither he nor they could believe how quickly (or how miraculously) God answered their prayers.

Type: Tandem storytelling

Tellers: Bonnie—A serious storyteller trying to tell the story correctly (female or male); George—Her friend, who keeps getting everything mixed up (male or female).

Tools: None

Topics: Angels, faith, freedom, God's power, Peter, prayer, worship

Tips: Both storytellers start onstage, or enter together. Bring up the stage lights, and then begin when the students are quiet.

Script:

Bonnie: One day, the king arrested James,

George: One of the apostles,

Bonnie: And had him—

George: Killed by the sword.

Bonnie: And when he saw how much it pleased the Jews—

George: He had Peter arrested, too.

Bonnie: Right in the middle of the Passover festival.

George: He stuck him in prison.

Bonnie: With sixteen soldiers guarding him.

George: That's a lot of manpower!

Bonnie: Right. And he planned to do the same thing to Peter as he'd done to James.

George: Yikes.

Bonnie: As soon as the festival was done.

George: But—

Bonnie: The church prayed for him. . . .

George: It doesn't look good for our hero. Will he escape? Will he be rescued? Will he meet the same fate as James? Tune in next week to find out. And don't miss another episode in this exciting miniseries. . .

Bonnie: What are you doing?

George: A little teaser for next week's episode.

Bonnie: We're not waiting until next week to finish telling this story.

George: We're not?

Bonnie:	No. We're gonna tell 'em the story right now.
George:	Oh. Are you sure?
Bonnie:	Yes!
George:	Can we break for a commercial or something?
Bonnie:	No.
George:	A word from our sponsors?
Bonnie:	We don't have any sponsors!
George:	A potty break?
Bonnie:	Look, Peter was in prison, right?
George:	Right!
Bonnie:	And as he sat in prison all during Passover, on the night before he was to be put on trial—
George:	U.S. Commandos stormed the prison, and led him through a secret underground passage to a submarine which was waiting to take him to a remote military base in Argentina—
Bonnie:	What you talking about?! That's not how the story goes!
George:	It's not? Oh. I must have looked at the wrong script. So, what happened next?
Bonnie:	He was chained between two soldiers and the other fourteen were on duty by the doors leading out of the prison. Suddenly, there was a bright light in the cell!
George:	Someone had turned on his flashlight!
Bonnie:	No. It was an—
George:	Alien!
Bonnie:	It was an angel!
George:	Oh. Wait a minute, how many cells were there?
Bonnie:	One.
George:	Do you know what they call a one-celled prison in Mexico?
Bonnie:	No. What?
George:	An amoeba.
Bonnie:	Could we get on with the story?
George:	Sure.
Bonnie:	The angel tapped him on the shoulder and said—
George:	"Wakey! Wakey! Rise and shine!"
Bonnie:	No—
George:	"Surprise! You're on candid camera!"
Bonnie:	No, the angel said, "Get up! Quick!" And as he stood up, the chains fell off his wrists!
George:	Cool.
Bonnie:	Then the angel said, "Grab your sandals and put on some clothes."
George:	He didn't have any clothes on!?
Bonnie:	He was wearing prison clothes.
George:	Could you see his bellybutton?
Bonnie:	No.
George:	Oh.
Bonnie:	"And grab your coat and come with me!"
George:	What about the guards?
Bonnie:	Huh?
George:	The guards, didn't they wake up or anything?
Bonnie:	Well, no.

George:	How come?
Bonnie:	God was in control the whole time.
George:	Oh. Cool.
Bonnie:	So, Peter followed the angel. They walked right past each set of guards until they came to the main door at the front of the prison. And the gate opened all by itself!
George:	Ah! Ghosts!
Bonnie:	No, not ghosts.
George:	Remote control.
Bonnie:	No.
George:	Motion sensors?
Bonnie:	The angel did it!
George:	Oh. Cool.
Bonnie:	As Peter was walking down the street, he thought it was all a dream until suddenly—
George:	The prison alarm went off! *(Make a loud siren sound)*
Bonnie:	No, the angel disappeared. Poof!
George:	Poof?
Bonnie:	Poof.
George:	Poof.
Bonnie:	Right, poof.
George:	*(Patting her on the shoulder)* Leave the sound effects to me. . .
Bonnie:	Okay.
George:	Great.
Bonnie:	And Peter said, "Wow! God has saved me! That was an angel!"
George:	Cool.
Bonnie:	And he went to John Mark's mom's house. Her name was Mary.
George:	Wait a minute. Lemme ask you a question.
Bonnie:	What's that?
George:	Why are there so many "Mary's" in the Bible? I mean, you've got Mary, the mother of Jesus; Mary of Magdala; Mary and Martha; and now Mary the mother of John Mark!
Bonnie:	It was a popular name back then.
George:	Why didn't they name their girls names like *(Choose names of the girls in your class, for example, "Amber, Chondra, Brianna, or Celeste?")*
Bonnie:	I don't know. Look, they went to the house and a whole lot of believers were inside praying.
George:	For Peter.
Bonnie:	Yeah, so he knocked on the door and this girl named Rhonda—
George:	Good. I thought you were gonna say Mary—
Bonnie:	Went to answer the door. And when she answered the door, she said,
George:	"No thanks! We gave at the office!"
Bonnie:	What?!
George:	I mean, "How much are the girl scout cookies, anyway?"
Bonnie:	No. She was so shocked, that it was really Peter—
George:	And not someone named Mary.
Bonnie:	That she didn't even invite him inside, she just ran back to everyone else and told them—
George:	"The pizza delivery guy is here. Whose got the money?"
Bonnie:	She said, "It's Peter at the door!"

George:	"No way!" they said. "You're crazy! He's in jail!"
Bonnie:	But she insisted. And then they thought maybe it was his angel.
George:	Huh?
Bonnie:	They thought maybe Peter's guardian angel had showed up at their door.
George:	Oh. Cool.
Bonnie:	So anyway, meanwhile, Peter was still standing out there, knocking on the door.
George:	And ringing the doorbell. *(Make doorbell sounds)* Brrring! Brrring! "Anybody home? Hello! *(Knock your fist against Bonnie's head and say in her ear)* Anybody home? Hello!"
Bonnie:	Stop that. Finally, they opened up the door and they were amazed to see Peter standing there. Just then he said—
George:	"Trick or Treat!"
Bonnie:	No, he told them to quiet down. And then he told them the whole story about how the angel led him out of the prison.
George:	Did he tell 'em the amoeba joke?
Bonnie:	Um. . . No.
George:	Too bad.
Bonnie:	And he told them to tell James about it—
George:	I thought James had been killed.
Bonnie:	This was a different James.
George:	I should have known. James and Mary, everywhere you look.
Bonnie:	At dawn, all the soldiers were like,
George:	*(Look around for Peter)* "Okay. Where is that guy? I know he was here a minute ago. . ."
Bonnie:	And the king ordered a manhunt. But they couldn't find Peter anywhere.
George:	So the king questioned the soldiers—
Bonnie:	Right. And when they couldn't tell him where Peter was, he sentenced them all to death.
George:	Yikes. This guy had some serious issues.
Bonnie:	You're telling me.
George:	And Peter escaped just like that?
Bonnie:	Yup. God heard the prayers of those people.
George:	And they couldn't even believe it when God answered their prayers!
Bonnie:	Even Peter thought it was all a dream at first.
George:	Does God still do that?
Bonnie:	What?
George:	Answer prayers?
Bonnie:	Sure. God's just as powerful today as he was back then. And he still answers the prayers of his followers when we pray believing that he hears us and cares about our needs.
George:	I have one thing to say about that.
Bonnie:	What's that? Lemme guess, "cool"?
George:	Nope. Awesome. . .. Very awesome.
Bonnie:	Right.
George:	And cool.

(Exit. Fade out the stage lights.)

The Breaking Jail
Jailbreak

Based On: Acts 16:16-36

Big Idea: God miraculously delivered Paul and Silas from prison.

Background: Paul and Silas, two missionaries in the early Christian church, became unpopular with the slave owners of a girl whom they set free from a demon. God orchestrated a way for them to be released from prison and to witness to the jail's warden and his family.

Type: Tandem storytelling with audience participation

Tellers: Bonnie—A serious storyteller trying to tell the story correctly (female or male); George—Her friend, who keeps getting everything mixed up (male or female).

Tools: None; optional—a can of shaving cream

Topics: Angels, conversion, courage, demons, faith, freedom, friendship, God's power, ministry, resentment, witnessing, worship

Tips: Both storytellers start onstage, or enter together. Bring up the stage lights, and then begin when the students are quiet.

Script

George: Once, Paul and Silas—

Bonnie: Two missionaries from the early Christian church—

George: Were walking to the place of prayer.

Bonnie: When suddenly—

George: A meteor fell from the sky and bonked them each on the head! *(Bonk yourself and Bonnie)*

Bonnie: What?!

George: There wasn't a meteor?

Bonnie: No.

George: UFOs and flying saucers?

Bonnie: No. There was just a girl.

George: A girl? That's it? They saw a girl falling from the sky!?

Bonnie: Walking on the ground. And, well, she was a slave.

George: Oh, that's not good.

Bonnie: And she was bugging them day and night.

George: That's really not good.

Bonnie: And she was possessed by a demon.

George: That's really, really not good.

Bonnie: But the thing was, this girl could predict the future.

George: What's so great about that?

Bonnie: What do you mean? That was amazing!

George: I can predict the future.

Bonnie: You can predict the future?

George:	Sure. I predict that I'm gonna mess up your hair! *(Mess up Bonnie's hair) (Optional section)* And I predict that I'm gonna use this can of shaving cream and draw a smiley face on your shirt! *(Draw the smiley face. End of optional section)*
Bonnie:	Stop that. Well, the girl didn't really predict the future, really it was the demon inside her that did. But her slave owners earned lots of money by having her do this.
George:	Hmm. . . So, she predicted the future. . . .
Bonnie:	Yup. And she followed Paul and Silas all over the place everywhere they went.
George:	*(Shocked)* Even into the boy's bathroom!
Bonnie:	Um, not there. But wherever she did follow them, she called out—
George:	"Peanuts! Popcorn! Get your red hots here!"
Bonnie:	She wasn't selling concessions! She was actually announcing who they were, "These men are servants of the Most High God! They are telling you how you can be saved!"
George:	Why would a demon say that? That stuff was true!
Bonnie:	Well, the demon certainly wasn't trying to get people to believe their message. Maybe he was making fun of them, maybe he was trying to show disrespect, in any case, it was bad advertising.
George:	What do you mean?
Bonnie:	Well, would you want a demon-possessed girl preaching at your church's next revival?
George:	Good point.
Bonnie:	So, finally, Paul turned to the girl and told the demon, "That's it! In the name of Jesus Christ, I order you to leave that girl alone!"
George:	Did it go?
Bonnie:	Yup.
George:	Did her head spin around in circles first?
Bonnie:	No. Actually, the demon left just like *(Snap your fingers)* that.
George:	Just like *(Snap your fingers)* that?
Bonnie:	Yup. Just like *(Snap your fingers again)* that.
George:	Wow. For these guys, casting out demons was a *(Snap your fingers again)* snap!
Bonnie:	Actually, for God it was a *(Snap your fingers again)* snap. On their own they couldn't do anything.
George:	Right. *(Snap your fingers again)*
Bonnie:	So, the demon left her alone. And then, she wasn't able to predict the future anymore.
George:	Whoa. I'll bet her slave owners weren't too happy about that!
Bonnie:	No, they weren't. In fact, they were so mad they grabbed Paul and Silas—
George:	And robbed 'em of every penny they had.
Bonnie:	No. But they did drag them to the police station—
George:	The police station?!
Bonnie:	Well, something just like it. And they told the city officials, "These guys are starting a riot! And not only that, but they're also telling the people of our city not to obey our laws!"
George:	That wasn't true, was it?
Bonnie:	No, of course not.
George:	Good. 'Cause I was hoping these were the good guys.
Bonnie:	They are. But a mob formed and the city leaders ordered that they be beaten!
George:	They beat the mob!
Bonnie:	They beat Silas and Paul. They were whipped and beaten.
George:	And scrambled and served sunny-side up.
Bonnie:	Look, this isn't funny! These guys were really tortured and punished. They were hurt very badly.

George: Oh. Sorry. It's just that you said they were whipped and beaten, and I got to thinking of eggs.

Bonnie: Okay.

George: And omelets.

Bonnie: I understand.

George: And egg salad sandwiches. And scrambled eggs, too.

Bonnie: I see.

George: And I wasn't trying to make fun of them. I'm sorry it sounded like that.

Bonnie: Okay, I forgive you. It's all over with.

George: Eggs-celent.

Bonnie: What?

George: Eggs-celent. Let's eggs-plain the rest of the story now. And give eggs-amples of the eggs-tent of God's power.

Bonnie: *(Sighing)* Then, they were thrown into prison. And the warden wanted to make sure they couldn't escape, so he stuck 'em in an inner cell and locked the doors. And clamped chains around their ankles.

George: Boy. Those guys are goners.

Bonnie: But that night, at about midnight—

George: Was there a full moon?

Bonnie: I don't know. It doesn't matter.

George: I wanted to make sure none of 'em were werewolves.

Bonnie: There aren't such things as werewolves! Now listen, at midnight, there was a great sound—

George: *(Howling like a werewolf)* Arrrrr!

Bonnie: Not that kind of sound.

George: Oh. "Peanuts! Popcorn! Get your red hots here!"

Bonnie: It was an earthquake.

George: Did they live in California?

Bonnie: No! Now, Paul and Silas had been singing hymns and praying as the other prisoners listened.

George: But when the earthquake came, they stopped.

Bonnie: Right!

George: Because the organist fell into a huge hole in the ground.

Bonnie: Look, there was no organist. But the prison was shaken and all the doors flew open! And all the chains fell off the prisoners!

George: *(Peering down into a great hole)* And into that giant gaping hole in the earth. . . . landing on top of the organist.

Bonnie: Then, the warden woke up, and when he saw that the doors were open, he figured that all the convicts had escaped.

George: And he freaked out.

Bonnie: Right. He pulled out his sword and was getting ready to kill himself—

George: Yikes! Why?

Bonnie: Well, back then if you were a guard at a jail and a prisoner escaped, they would put you to death.

George: Whoa. That guy's a goner.

Bonnie: But Paul put out his hand and said, "Stop!—"

George: *(Singing)* "In the name of love! Before you stab your heart!"

Bonnie: "We're all still here! Don't hurt yourself!"

George: *(Singing)* "Think it over!"

Bonnie:	*(Shake your head)*
George:	Why hadn't the prisoners run away?
Bonnie:	Well, they probably figured the God of Paul and Silas was calling the shots and they didn't wanna mess with him.
George:	Smart choice.
Bonnie:	No kidding. And the jailer was shaking. He called for some lights.
George:	Was the electricity out because of the earthquake?
Bonnie:	Electricity wasn't invented yet!
George:	Oh, yeah that's right.
Bonnie:	And then he ran over and fell down, scared, at Paul and Silas's feet. And he asked them, "Sirs! What must I do to be saved?!"
George:	Aha! He remembered.
Bonnie:	He remembered what?
George:	Why they'd been thrown in prison in the first place—remember the girl with the demon?
Bonnie:	Yeah.
George:	Well, that's what she was telling everyone! That these two men could tell people how to be saved. Remember?
Bonnie:	Wow! You're right. Good memory!
George:	And so, Paul and Silas told him, "Believe in the Lord Jesus and you'll be saved!"
Bonnie:	Right again! Then, they told him all about the good news of Jesus and he and his whole family believed.
George:	Then, they all got baptized, right?
Bonnie:	Yup. After the warden helped put bandages on Paul and Silas' wounds.
George:	Were they Arthur *(or another popular cartoon personality)* Band-Aids?
Bonnie:	No. Then they all had a great big meal to celebrate.
George:	As brothers and sisters in the family of God!
Bonnie:	Right. And in the morning, the city officials ordered that he release Paul and Silas.
George:	Even though it was the jailer and his family who'd been set free!
Bonnie:	What do you mean?
George:	Free from sin. And he told them, "You're free to leave. Go in peace!"
Bonnie:	Yup, and can you sum up the big idea of this story?
George:	Never visit California during an earthquake!
Bonnie:	What?
George:	Werewolves don't like to sing organ music?
Bonnie:	Look, the big idea is that we can believe in Jesus, too.
George:	Just like that jailer did—
Bonnie:	And be set free.
George:	Just like that jailer was.
Bonnie:	And go home in peace.
George:	To eat some scrambled eggs.
Together:	The end.

(Bow. Exit. Fade out the stage lights.)

Scripture Verse Index

Old Testament Verses

Genesis 1-2: "The World's First Artist"

Genesis 3: "The Day Sin Came In"

Genesis 4: "Cain Wasn't Abel"

Genesis 6-9: "The Flood"

Genesis 12-25: "Abraham—Father of the Faithful"*

Genesis 37-50: "Joseph—The Prince of Dreams"*

Genesis 37, 39: "The Dreamer (the story of Joseph, act 1)"

Genesis 40-41: "The Rise of Zappo (the story of Joseph, act 2)"

Genesis 42-45: "The Family Reunion (the story of Joseph, act 3)"

Genesis 50: "The Family Reunion (the story of Joseph, act 3)"

Exodus 1-20: "Moses—The Desert Prince"*

Exodus 1-2:10: "The Kayak Kid"

Exodus 5-12: "The Master of Disasters"

Exodus 32-34: "Moses—The Desert Prince"*

Numbers 13-14 : "Joshua—God's Spy Guy"*

Deuteronomy 31:1-8 : "Joshua—God's Spy Guy"*

Joshua 1: "Joshua—God's Spy Guy"*

Joshua 2: "Rahab—The Daring Outcast"*

Judges 4-5: "Deborah—Woman Warrior"*

Judges 6-7: "Gideon—An Unlikely Hero"*

Judges 13-16: "Samson—Real-life Superhero"*

Ruth (entire book): "Ruth—Dutiful Daughter-in-law"*

1 Samuel 13:14: "David—The Giant-slayer"*

1 Samuel 16-17: "David—The Giant-slayer"*

1 Samuel 17: "The Giant Match-up"

1 Kings 3: "Solomon—The World's Wisest Wisher"*

1 Kings 17-18: "Elijah—Man of Miracles"*

2 Kings 2:1-18: "Elijah—Man of Miracles"*

Nehemiah (entire book): "Nehemiah—The Prayerful Planner"*

Esther (entire book): "Esther—The Courageous Beauty Queen"*

Ecclesiastes 12:13: "Solomon—The World's Wisest Wisher"*

Daniel 1, 6: "Daniel—The Powerful Praying Prophet"*

New Testament Verses

Matthew (entire book): "Jesus—Child of Mary, Son of God"*

Matthew 3: "The Baptism of Jesus", "John the Baptist—Forerunner to Jesus"*

Matthew 4:18-20: "Peter—The Pebble Who Became a Rock"*

Matthew 4:21-22: "John—Friend of Jesus"*

Matthew 11:1-19: "John the Baptist—Forerunner to Jesus"*

Matthew 14:22-33 : "Peter—The Pebble Who Became a Rock"*

Matthew 16:18: "Peter—The Pebble Who Became a Rock"*

Matthew 17:1-9: "John—Friend of Jesus"*

Matthew 26:69-75 : "Peter—The Pebble Who Became a Rock"*

Mark (entire book) : "Jesus—Child of Mary, Son of God"*

Mark 1:12-13: "No Dessert in the Desert"

Mark 2:1-12: "Rappelling Through the Roof"

Mark 5:1-20: "A Graveyard Story"

Mark 16: "At the Scene of the Grave"

Luke (entire book) : "Jesus—Child of Mary, Son of God"*

Luke 2:1-20: "Unidentified Flying Angels"

Luke 2:41-52: "The Missing Mini-Messiah"

Luke 3:1-22: "The Baptism of Jesus"

Luke 4:1-13: "No Dessert in the Desert"

Luke 5:1-11: "www.greatbig-fishcatch.net"

Luke 10:38-42: "Mary—Follower of Jesus"*

Luke 22:7-23: "The Last Supper"

John (entire book): "Jesus—Child of Mary, Son of God"*

John 11:1-45: "Mary—Follower of Jesus"*

John 12:1-11: "Mary—Follower of Jesus"*

John 13:18-28: "John—Friend of Jesus"*

John 13:21-30: "The Last Supper"

John 18:1-11: "Peter—The Pebble Who Became a Rock"*

John 20:1-18: "At the Scene of the Grave"

Acts 2: "Tongues of Fire"

Acts 2:14-41 : "Peter—The Pebble Who Became a Rock"*

Acts 3:1-10 : "Peter—The Pebble Who Became a Rock"*

Acts 6:8-8: "Stephen—The First Christian Martyr"*

Acts 9:1-31: "Paul—Preacher to the World"*

Acts 9:36-43: "When Tabitha Got Sew Sick. . . She Dyed"

Acts 10-11:18: "Dinner Reservations"

Acts 10:43: "Dinner Reservations"

Acts 12:1-2: "John—Friend of Jesus"*

Acts 12:1-19: "Who Can That Be Knocking at My Door?"

Acts 12:12: "Jesus—Child of Mary, Son of God"*

Acts 16:16-36: "The Breaking Jail Jailbreak"

Acts 17:27 : "Paul—Preacher to the World"*

Acts 18:1-3: "Priscilla and Aquila—A Couple of Leaders"*

Acts 18:18-28: "Priscilla and Aquila—A Couple of Leaders"*

Romans 4:16-17: "Abraham—Father of the Faithful"*

Romans 6:1-11 : "Paul—Preacher to the World"*

Romans 7:15-25 : "Paul—Preacher to the World"*

Romans 16:3-4 : "Priscilla and Aquila—A Couple of Leaders"*

1 Corinthians 1:18-31 : "Paul—Preacher to the World"*

1 Corinthians 1:27: "Paul—Preacher to the World"*

1 Corinthians 16:19: "Priscilla and Aquila—A Couple of Leaders"*

2 Corinthians 11:26-27: "Paul—Preacher to the World"*

2 Corinthians 12:10 : "Paul—Preacher to the World"*

Galatians 1:17-18: "Paul—Preacher to the World"*

Galatians 2:20: "Paul—Preacher to the World"*

Ephesians 2:1-11: "Paul—Preacher to the World"*

Ephesians 6:21-22 : "Priscilla and Aquila—A Couple of Leaders"*

Philippians 1:21: "Paul—Preacher to the World"*

Colossians 4:7-9: "Priscilla and Aquila—A Couple of Leaders"*

Hebrews 11: "Hebrews 11—God's Faith Hall of Fame"*

Hebrews 11:8-19: "Abraham—Father of the Faithful"*

Hebrews 11:31: "Rahab—The Daring Outcast"*

Hebrews 11:32: "Samson—Real-life Superhero"*

James 2:24-25: "Rahab—The Daring Outcast"*

1 John 3:18: "John—Friend of Jesus"*

* Appears in *24 Tandem Bible Hero Storyscripts for Children's Ministry*

Story Type Index

Tandem Storytelling

Abraham—Father of the Faithful*

Deborah—Woman Warrior*

Gideon—An Unlikely Hero*

David—The Giant-slayer*

Solomon—The World's Wisest Wisher*

Elijah—Man of Miracles*

Esther—The Courageous Beauty Queen*

John the Baptist—Forerunner to Jesus*

John—Friend of Jesus*

Stephen—The First Christian Martyr*

Priscilla and Aquila—A Couple of Leaders*

Hebrews 11—God's Faith Hall of Fame*

The World's First Artist

The Day Sin Came In

Cain Wasn't Abel

The Flood

The Dreamer (the story of Joseph, act 1)

The Rise of Zappo (the story of Joseph, act 2)

The Family Reunion (the story of Joseph, act 3)

The Kayak Kid

The Baptism of Jesus

Rappelling Through the Roof

Tongues of Fire

When Tabitha Got Sew Sick. . . She Dyed

Who Can That Be Knocking at My Door?

The Breaking Jail Jailbreak

Tandem Monologues

Joseph—The Prince of Dreams*

Moses—The Desert Prince*

Nehemiah—The Prayerful Planner*

Mary—Follower of Jesus*

The Master of Disasters

A Graveyard Story

Dinner Reservations

Narralogue

Joshua—God's Spy Guy*

Gideon—An Unlikely Hero*

Samson—Real-life Superhero*

Jesus—Child of Mary, Son of God*

No Dessert in the Desert

The Last Supper

Storymime

Moses—The Desert Prince*

Elijah—Man of Miracles*

The Master of Disasters

www.greatbigfishcatch.net

Interview

Rahab—The Daring Outcast*

Ruth—Dutiful Daughter-in-law*

Paul—Preacher to the World*

Unidentified Flying Angels

The Missing Mini-Messiah

At the Scene of the Grave

Sports Announcer

Daniel—The Powerful Praying Prophet*

Peter—The Pebble Who Became a Rock*

The Giant Match-up

* Appears in *24 Tandem Bible Hero Storyscripts for Children's Ministry*

Topical Index

Anger
Cain Wasn't Abel

Angels
Gideon—An Unlikely Hero*
Daniel—The Powerful Praying
  Prophet*
Unidentified Flying Angels
No Dessert in the Desert
Dinner Reservations
Who Can That Be Knocking at
  My Door?
The Breaking Jail Jailbreak

Baptism
John the Baptist—Forerunner to
  Jesus*
The Baptism of Jesus
Tongues of Fire

Bullies
Joseph—The Prince of
  Dreams*
David—The Giant-slayer*
The Dreamer
The Giant Match-up

Calling
Abraham—Father of the
  Faithful*
Moses—The Desert Prince*
Gideon—An Unlikely Hero*
Elijah—Man of Miracles*
Jesus—Child of Mary, Son of
  God*
Hebrews 11—God's Faith Hall
  of Fame*
The Kayak Kid
www.greatbigfishcatch.net

Choices
Abraham—Father of the
  Faithful*
Rahab—The Daring Outcast*
Solomon—The World's Wisest
  Wisher*
Esther—The Courageous
  Beauty Queen*

Nehemiah—The Prayerful
  Planner*
The Day Sin Came In
No Dessert in the Desert

Christmas
Jesus—Child of Mary, Son of
  God*
Unidentified Flying Angels

Confession
Stephen—The First Christian
  Martyr*
www.greatbigfishcatch.net

Consequences
Hebrews 11—God's Faith Hall
  of Fame*
The Day Sin Came In
Cain Wasn't Abel
The Flood
The Master of Disasters

Conversion
Rahab—The Daring Outcast*
Ruth—Dutiful Daughter-in-
  law*
John the Baptist—Forerunner to
  Jesus*
Paul—Preacher to the World*
Hebrews 11—God's Faith Hall
  of Fame*
The Baptism of Jesus
A Graveyard Story
Tongues of Fire
Dinner Reservations
The Breaking Jail Jailbreak

Conviction
Daniel—The Powerful Praying
  Prophet*
Esther—The Courageous
  Beauty Queen*
Nehemiah—The Prayerful
  Planner*
Mary—Follower of Jesus*
Stephen—The First Christian
  Martyr*

Paul—Preacher to the World*
Hebrews 11—God's Faith Hall
  of Fame*
The Giant Match-up
No Dessert in the Desert

Courage
Abraham—Father of the
  Faithful*
Moses—The Desert Prince*
Joshua—God's Spy Guy*
Rahab—The Daring Outcast*
Deborah—Woman Warrior*
Gideon—An Unlikely Hero*
Samson—Real-life Superhero*
David—The Giant-slayer*
Elijah—Man of Miracles*
Daniel—The Powerful Praying
  Prophet*
Esther—The Courageous
  Beauty Queen*
Nehemiah—The Prayerful
  Planner*
Jesus—Child of Mary, Son of
  God*
Peter—The Pebble Who
  Became a Rock*
Stephen—The First Christian
  Martyr*
Paul—Preacher to the World*
Priscilla and Aquila—A Couple
  of Leaders*
Hebrews 11—God's Faith Hall
  of Fame*
The Dreamer
The Master of Disasters
The Giant Match-up
The Breaking Jail Jailbreak

Creation
The World's First Artist

Death
Ruth—Dutiful Daughter-in-
  law*
Stephen—The First Christian
  Martyr*

The Day Sin Came In
When Tabitha Got Sew Sick. . .
    She Dyed

Demons
The Day Sin Came In
No Dessert in the Desert
A Graveyard Story
The Breaking Jail Jailbreak

Disappointment
Ruth—Dutiful Daughter-in-
    law*
Hebrews 11—God's Faith Hall
    of Fame*

Doubt
John the Baptist—Forerunner to
    Jesus*
Peter—The Pebble Who
    Became a Rock*

Dreams
Joseph—The Prince of
    Dreams*
Solomon—The World's Wisest
    Wisher*
Daniel—The Powerful Praying
    Prophet*
The Dreamer
The Rise of Zappo

Easter
Jesus—Child of Mary, Son of
    God*
Mary—Follower of Jesus*
At the Scene of the Grave

Evangelism
(See Witnessing)

Excuses
The Day Sin Came In
Cain Wasn't Abel

Faith
Abraham—Father of the
    Faithful*
Ruth—Dutiful Daughter-in-
    law*
David—The Giant-slayer*
Elijah—Man of Miracles*
Daniel—The Powerful Praying

Prophet*
Nehemiah—The Prayerful
    Planner*
John the Baptist—Forerunner to
    Jesus*
Peter—The Pebble Who
    Became a Rock*
Mary—Follower of Jesus*
Stephen—The First Christian
    Martyr*
Hebrews 11—God's Faith Hall
    of Fame*
The Day Sin Came In
The Flood
The Rise of Zappo
The Giant Match-up
Rappelling Through the Roof
The Last Supper
When Tabitha Got Sew Sick. . .
    She Dyed
Dinner Reservations
Who Can That Be Knocking at
    My Door?
The Breaking Jail Jailbreak

Faithfulness
Deborah—Woman Warrior*
Ruth—Dutiful Daughter-in-
    law*
Elijah—Man of Miracles*
John the Baptist—Forerunner to
    Jesus*
Priscilla and Aquila—A Couple
    of Leaders*

Family Relationships
Joseph—The Prince of
    Dreams*
Ruth—Dutiful Daughter-in-
    law*
Esther—The Courageous
    Beauty Queen*
Cain Wasn't Abel
The Dreamer
The Family Reunion
The Kayak Kid
The Missing Mini-Messiah

Following God
Abraham—Father of the
    Faithful*

Moses—The Desert Prince*
Gideon—An Unlikely Hero*
Samson—Real-life Superhero*
David—The Giant-slayer*
Solomon—The World's Wisest
    Wisher*
Esther—The Courageous
    Beauty Queen*
Nehemiah—The Prayerful
    Planner*
Jesus—Child of Mary, Son of
    God*
Peter—The Pebble Who
    Became a Rock*
John—Friend of Jesus*
Mary—Follower of Jesus*
Stephen—The First Christian
    Martyr*
Paul—Preacher to the World*
Hebrews 11—God's Faith Hall
    of Fame*
The Flood
The Missing Mini-Messiah
The Baptism of Jesus
No Dessert in the Desert
A Graveyard Story
www.greatbigfishcatch.net
Dinner Reservations

Forgiveness
Joseph—The Prince of
    Dreams*
Jesus—Child of Mary, Son of
    God*
Stephen—The First Christian
    Martyr*
Paul—Preacher to the World*
The Day Sin Came In
The Family Reunion
Rappelling Through the Roof
The Last Supper
Dinner Reservations

Freedom
Moses—The Desert Prince*
Gideon—An Unlikely Hero*
The Master of Disasters
A Graveyard Story
Who Can That Be Knocking at
    My Door?

The Breaking Jail Jailbreak

Friendship
Elijah—Man of Miracles*
John—Friend of Jesus*
Mary—Follower of Jesus*
Priscilla and Aquila—A Couple of Leaders*
Rappelling Through the Roof
The Last Supper
When Tabitha Got Sew Sick. . . She Dyed
The Breaking Jail Jailbreak

Generosity
Mary—Follower of Jesus*
When Tabitha Got Sew Sick. . . She Dyed
Dinner Reservations

Giftedness
Deborah—Woman Warrior*
Samson—Real-life Superhero*
Solomon—The World's Wisest Wisher*
The Giant Match-up

God's Existence
John the Baptist—Forerunner to Jesus*
The World's First Artist

God's Love
John—Friend of Jesus*
Mary—Follower of Jesus*
The Day Sin Came In
The Dreamer
Unidentified Flying Angels
At the Scene of the Grave

God's Power
Joshua—God's Spy Guy*
Gideon—An Unlikely Hero*
The World's First Artist
The Flood
The Master of Disasters
The Giant Match-up
A Graveyard Story
www.greatbigfishcatch.net
Rappelling Through the Roof
When Tabitha Got Sew Sick. . . She Dyed

Who Can That Be Knocking at My Door?
The Breaking Jail Jailbreak

God's Sovereignty
Joseph—The Prince of Dreams*
Moses—The Desert Prince*
Ruth—Dutiful Daughter-in-law*
Daniel—The Powerful Praying Prophet*
Hebrews 11—God's Faith Hall of Fame*
The Rise of Zappo
The Family Reunion
The Kayak Kid

God's word
John the Baptist—Forerunner to Jesus*
Stephen—The First Christian Martyr*
Paul—Preacher to the World*
Priscilla and Aquila—A Couple of Leaders*
The Missing Mini-Messiah
No Dessert in the Desert

Grace
Jesus—Child of Mary, Son of God*
Paul—Preacher to the World*
Hebrews 11—God's Faith Hall of Fame*
The Day Sin Came In
At the Scene of the Grave
Dinner Reservations

Grief and Loss
Ruth—Dutiful Daughter-in-law*
When Tabitha Got Sew Sick. . . She Dyed

Hiding
The Day Sin Came In

Holy Spirit
Gideon—An Unlikely Hero*
Samson—Real-life Superhero*
Elijah—Man of Miracles*

Stephen—The First Christian Martyr*
The Baptism of Jesus
Tongues of Fire
Dinner Reservations

Hope
Esther—The Courageous Beauty Queen*
John the Baptist—Forerunner to Jesus*
Stephen—The First Christian Martyr*
Hebrews 11—God's Faith Hall of Fame*
Unidentified Flying Angels

Jealousy
Joseph—The Prince of Dreams*
Daniel—The Powerful Praying Prophet*
Cain Wasn't Abel
The Dreamer

Jesus
John the Baptist—Forerunner to Jesus*
Jesus—Child of Mary, Son of God*
John—Friend of Jesus*
Mary—Follower of Jesus*
Unidentified Flying Angels
The Missing Mini-Messiah
The Baptism of Jesus
No Dessert in the Desert
A Graveyard Story
www.greatbigfishcatch.net
Rappelling Through the Roof
The Last Supper
At the Scene of the Grave

Judas
The Last Supper

Leadership
Moses—The Desert Prince
Deborah—Woman Warrior*
Samson—Real-life Superhero*
Peter—The Pebble Who Became a Rock*
Priscilla and Aquila—A Couple

of Leaders*
The Family Reunion

Listening
Abraham—Father of the
   Faithful*
The Master of Disasters
Unidentified Flying Angels

Lord's Supper
John—Friend of Jesus*
The Last Supper

Ministry
Elijah—Man of Miracles*
John the Baptist—Forerunner to
   Jesus*
Jesus—Child of Mary, Son of
   God*
Stephen—The First Christian
   Martyr*
Paul—Preacher to the World*
Priscilla and Aquila—A Couple
   of Leaders*
Hebrews 11—God's Faith Hall
   of Fame*
The Baptism of Jesus
www.greatbigfishcatch.net
The Breaking Jail Jailbreak

New Life
Jesus—Child of Mary, Son of
   God*
Mary—Follower of Jesus*
Paul—Preacher to the World*
Hebrews 11—God's Faith Hall
   of Fame*
The Baptism of Jesus
A Graveyard Story
At the Scene of the Grave
When Tabitha Got Sew Sick. . .
   She Dyed

Obedience
Abraham—Father of the
   Faithful*
Joshua—God's Spy Guy*
Rahab—The Daring Outcast*
Ruth—Dutiful Daughter-in-
   law*
Jesus—Child of Mary, Son of

God*
Peter—The Pebble Who
   Became a Rock*
Hebrews 11—God's Faith Hall
   of Fame*
The Day Sin Came In
The Flood
The Master of Disasters
The Baptism of Jesus
No Dessert in the Desert

Patience
David—The Giant-slayer
The Rise of Zappo

Passover
Moses—The Desert Prince*
Master of Disasters
The Last Supper

Pentecost
Tongues of Fire

Perseverance
Hebrews 11—God's Faith Hall
   of Fame*

Peter
Peter—The Pebble Who
   Became a Rock*
Tongues of Fire
When Tabitha Got Sew Sick. . .
   She Dyed
Dinner Reservations
Who Can That Be Knocking at
   My Door?

Planning
Joshua—God's Spy Guy*
Nehemiah—The Prayerful
   Planner*

Prayer
Samson—Real-life Superhero*
David—The Giant-slayer*
Elijah—Man of Miracles*
Daniel—The Powerful Praying
   Prophet*
Nehemiah—The Prayerful
   Planner*
Jesus—Child of Mary, Son of
   God*

When Tabitha Got Sew Sick. . .
   She Dyed
Who Can That Be Knocking at
   My Door?

Prejudice
Dinner Reservations

Priorities
Solomon—The World's Wisest
   Wisher*
Daniel—The Powerful Praying
   Prophet*
John—Friend of Jesus*
Mary—Follower of Jesus*
Stephen—The First Christian
   Martyr*
Paul—Preacher to the World*
The Missing Mini-Messiah
No Dessert in the Desert
Rappelling Through the Roof

Prophecy Fulfillment
Jesus—Child of Mary, Son of
   God*
Stephen—The First Christian
   Martyr*
The Master of Disasters
Unidentified Flying Angels
At the Scene of the Grave
Tongues of Fire

Purpose
Joseph—The Prince of
   Dreams*
Deborah—Woman Warrior*
Samson—Real-life Superhero*
Ruth—Dutiful Daughter-in-
   law*
Daniel—The Powerful Praying
   Prophet*
Esther—The Courageous
   Beauty Queen*
Nehemiah—The Prayerful
   Planner*
John the Baptist—Forerunner to
   Jesus*
Paul—Preacher to the World*
The Rise of Zappo
The Missing Mini-Messiah
www.greatbigfishcatch.net

Questions
Ruth—Dutiful Daughter-in-law*
The Dreamer

Rebellion
Cain Wasn't Abel
The Flood

Repentance
Elijah—Man of Miracles*
John the Baptist—Forerunner to Jesus*
The Baptism of Jesus
Tongues of Fire

Resentment
Gideon—An Unlikely Hero*
Ruth—Dutiful Daughter-in-law*
Cain Wasn't Abel
The Dreamer
The Breaking Jail Jailbreak

Rest
Hebrews 11—God's Faith Hall of Fame*
The World's First Artist

Second Chances
Moses—The Desert Prince*
Joshua—God's Spy Guy*
Samson—Real-life Superhero*
The Day Sin Came In
The Flood
The Master of Disasters

Self-control
Nehemiah—The Prayerful Planner*
Cain Wasn't Abel
No Dessert in the Desert

Sin
Paul—Preacher to the World
The Day Sin Came In
Cain Wasn't Abel

The Flood
www.greatbigfishcatch.net
The Last Supper

Stubbornness
Cain Wasn't Abel
The Master of Disasters

Success
Deborah—Woman Warrior*
Gideon—An Unlikely Hero*
Samson—Real-life Superhero*
David—The Giant-slayer*
Solomon—The World's Wisest Wisher*
Nehemiah—The Prayerful Planner*
John the Baptist—Forerunner to Jesus*
The Giant Match-up

Suffering
Ruth—Dutiful Daughter-in-law*
Stephen—The First Christian Martyr*
Paul—Preacher to the World*
Hebrews 11—God's Faith Hall of Fame*
The Dreamer
The Rise of Zappo
The Family Reunion

Temptation
The Day Sin Came In
Cain Wasn't Abel
No Dessert in the Desert

Vengeance
Samson—Real-life Superhero*
Cain Wasn't Abel

Witnessing
Elijah—Man of Miracles*
John the Baptist—Forerunner to Jesus*

Peter—The Pebble Who Became a Rock*
John—Friend of Jesus*
Stephen—The First Christian Martyr*
Paul—Preacher to the World*
Priscilla and Aquila—A Couple of Leaders*
Hebrews 11—God's Faith Hall of Fame*
Unidentified Flying Angels
A Graveyard Story
Tongues of Fire
Dinner Reservations
The Breaking Jail Jailbreak

Worship
David—The Giant-slayer*
Daniel—The Powerful Praying Prophet*
Nehemiah—The Prayerful Planner*
Jesus—Child of Mary, Son of God*
Mary—Follower of Jesus*
Hebrews 11—God's Faith Hall of Fame*
Unidentified Flying Angels
The Last Supper
Dinner Reservations
Who Can That Be Knocking at My Door?
The Breaking Jail Jailbreak

* Appears in *24 Tandem Bible Hero Storyscripts for Children's Ministry*